The Uncounted

For MAP – without whom I would, of course, be lost

The Uncounted

Alex Cobham

polity

First published in 2020 by Polity Press

Polity Press
65 Bridge Street
Cambridge CB2 1UR, UK

Polity Press
101 Station Landing
Suite 300
Medford, MA 02155, USA

ISBN-13: 978-1-5095-3601-6
ISBN-13: 978-1-5095-3602-3 (pb)

A catalogue record for this book is available from the British Library.

Library of Congress Cataloging-in-Publication Data
Names: Cobham, Alex, author.
Title: The uncounted / Alex Cobham.
Description: Cambridge, UK ; Medford, MA, USA : Polity, 2020. | Includes
    bibliographical references and index. | Summary: "What we count matters,
    and in a world where policies and decisions are underpinned by numbers,
    statistics and data, if you're not counted, you don't count. In this
    book, Alex Cobham argues that systematic gaps in economic and
    demographic data not only lead us to understate a wide range of damaging
    inequalities, but also to actively exacerbate them"-- Provided by
    publisher.
Identifiers: LCCN 2019023983 (print) | LCCN 2019023984 (ebook) | ISBN
    9781509536016 (hardback) | ISBN 9781509536023 (paperback) | ISBN
    9781509536030 (epub)
Subjects: LCSH: Equality. | Population--Statistical methods. | Social
    sciences--Statistical methods. | Social indicators.
Classification: LCC HM821 .C634 2020 (print) | LCC HM821 (ebook) | DDC
    305--dc23
LC record available at https://lccn.loc.gov/2019023983
LC ebook record available at https://lccn.loc.gov/2019023984

Typeset in 11 on 13 pt Sabon by Servis Filmsetting Ltd, Stockport, Cheshire
Printed and bound in Great Britain by TJ International Limited

For further information on Polity, visit our website: politybooks.com

Contents

Preface

In late 1998, I sat down nervously at my first academic job interview, at Queen Elizabeth House (QEH, Oxford University's Department of International Development). As I mumbled about the model of multinational companies' location decisions that I'd been working on, I didn't realize that the two people interviewing me would come to form something like intellectual bookends for a quite different research path: that of the 'Uncounted'. Shamefully, I knew nothing of their work – not the leading work of Professor Frances Stewart on approaches to poverty and on group inequalities, nor that of Professor Valpy FitzGerald on tax havens and other issues of international finance and development. But one way and another, their work underpins the concept of the uncounted, at the bottom and at the top of the distribution, respectively.

The uncounted is the kind of idea that, once it's in your head, you find yourself seeing everywhere. At least I did. And so this book is a distillation of much of the work I've been lucky enough to be part of since that QEH interview. I am grateful to each of the organizations that have given me the chance, and each of the people who supported it, facilitated it, tolerated it, inspired it, turned a blind eye to it ...

These include QEH and St Anne's College, Oxford, where I was lucky to work with many dedicated colleagues and exceptional students; Christian Aid, where, with Charles Abugre, Alison Kelly and a host of talented campaign, media and advocacy staff, we launched the first international nongovernmental organization (INGO) campaign for tax justice, and encountered everything from the false outrage of Jersey's financial services sector at being accused of less than saintly practices, to the true outrage of the racist citizenship machinations of the Dominican Republic's government; Save the Children, where a committed team including Nuria Molina, Jess Espey and Alison Holder was able to make an important, progressive contribution to the UN discussions of the post-2015 agenda, and where a blog called 'Uncounted' first appeared; and the Center for Global Development, where Owen Barder and I provided technical input to the UK's 2013 G8 summit focused on tax transparency, and where Andy Sumner and I proposed the Palma ratio as an alternative income inequality measure (and a special mention to Charles Kenny, who fully deserves some of the blame for encouraging me to write this book).

I've also benefited from working with the International Centre for Tax and Development, where, with Mick Moore's important support and the dedication of Wilson Prichard and Andrew Goodall, the Government Revenue Database, now hosted at UNU-WIDER, was launched; the UN Global Thematic Consultation on Addressing Inequalities, where I was a moderator for the post-2015 economic inequalities discussion; the African Union/UNECA High Level Panel chaired by Thabo Mbeki, where Alice Lépissier and I proposed a new approach to illicit financial flows; the Fair Tax Mark, where an initiative to commend companies that embrace tax transparency was first launched; the Global Reporting Initiative, where I joined the technical committee drafting a tax transparency standard; the Independent Commission for the Reform of International Corporate Taxation (ICRICT), which is playing an important role in changing global norms; and (while I had the legs for it) Union Street FC, which is probably not.

While some roles focused more heavily on research, and some on public advocacy, the Tax Justice Network provides the happy freedom to pursue both. The network was formally established in 2003 to fight for a more equal global distribution of taxing rights, and with it the fair and effective tax systems that support powerful and inclusive human progress; and against the financial secrecy and unjust international rule-setting that thwarts this. Through rigorous analysis, expert policy engagement and high-profile public communications, we aim to promote radical proposals reflecting social justice concerns within what can otherwise often be closed, technical processes.

This book looks at both sides of a puzzle, to which tax justice is – naturally! – an important element of the answer. The first part of the book explores the ways in which people are excluded from political power directly, and from political *weighting* in decisions about public policy priorities. A fair tax system is part and parcel of ensuring transparent and accountable government, and inclusive political representation that weighs each person appropriately. The second part of the book deals with the top end of the income distribution – the analysis of financial secrecy and opacity that allows wealthy individuals and multinational companies to escape the onshore regulation and taxation that everyone else accepts as part of the social contract. Finally, the book concludes with a set of policy proposals. These, of course, draw heavily on the work of the amazing team and associated experts of the Tax Justice Network – to which any and all proceeds of the book will go. There are too many giants to name all the shoulders I'm standing on, many of whom are referenced through the text. John Christensen, erstwhile economic adviser to the secrecy jurisdiction of Jersey and subsequently founder of the Tax Justice Network, deserves enormous credit for turning ideas into movement.

I am grateful to all those individuals and organizations mentioned, and many more – from collaborators in catalytic efforts such as Open Data for Tax Justice, to our allies at the Global Alliance for Tax Justice and the Financial Transparency Coalition, to all those at UN bodies, including UNCTAD, UNECA, DESA and UNESCWA, who have participated in the ongoing efforts to achieve tax transparency and fairer international rules, and indeed some at the IMF, OECD and World Bank; and to the funders who have supported this work, including the Joffe Charitable Trust, Ford Foundation (where Rakesh Rajani was catalytic, for me personally as well as for TJN) and Norad. I'm grateful too for the insightful comments of Maria Moreno and two anonymous referees, the support of George Owers, Julia Davies and Sarah Dancy at Polity, Catherine Cobham and David Cobham, and the expert input of Dr Julia Prest in translating some seventeenth-century French, to Brooke Harrington and STEP for assistance with a reference, to Save the Children for permission to use and adapt figures to all those who have helped me find data, including Mikelyn Meyers and Cordell Golden, and to all the audiences everywhere who have ever sat through bits of this and improved the arguments and evidence with their comments and criticisms.

The late Joel Joffe was Nelson Mandela's lawyer during the Rivonia Trial, and described by Mandela as 'the General behind the scenes in our defence'. In a lifetime fighting the created injustices of apartheid and poverty, Joel was a champion of tax justice, and the Joffe Charitable Trust provided crucial financial support to the Tax Justice Network at a vital time. As someone who stood up to be counted, time and again, I hope Joel would have appreciated how the core argument of *The Uncounted* runs from the injustices of marginalization and oppression to those of tax abuse and exploitation – and offers some ways to start fighting back against them all.

Abbreviations

ACS	American Community Survey
BEPS	Base Erosion and Profit Shifting
CEMD	Confidential Enquiry into Maternal Deaths (UK)
CIPOLD	Confidential Inquiry into Premature Deaths of People with Learning Disabilities (UK)
CPI	Corruption Perceptions Index
CRISE	Centre for Research into Inequality, Security and Ethnicity
DFID	Department for International Development (UK)
DGE	Directoria Geral de Estatística (Brazil)
DTP3	diphtheria, tetanus, and pertussis
ECOSOC	Economic and Social Council (UN)
EITI	Extractive Industries Transparency Initiative
EU	European Union
FATCA	Foreign Account Tax Compliance Act (US)
FSI	Financial Secrecy Index
GAVI	Global Alliance on Vaccinations and Immunizations
GDP	gross domestic product
GFI	Global Financial Integrity

GRD   Government Revenue Dataset
GRID   Group Inequalities Database
ICIJ   International Consortium of Investigative
          Journalists
ICRICT   Independent Commission for the Reform of
          International Corporate Taxation
ICTD   International Centre for Tax and
          Development
IFF   illicit financial flows
ILO   International Labour Organization
IMF   International Monetary Fund
INGO   international nongovernmental
          organization
IPC   Integrated Food Security and Humanitarian
          Phase Classification Framework
ITIC   International Tax and Investment Center
JEM   Justice and Equality Movement (Sudan)
LeDeR   Learning Disabilities Mortality Review
LGBT   lesbian, gay, bisexual and transgender
MDGs   Millennium Development Goals
MNEs   multinational enterprises
NGO   nongovernmental organization
NHS   National Health Service (UK)
OECD   Organization for Economic Cooperation and
          Development
ONS   Office for National Statistics (UK)
OPHI   Oxford Poverty and Human Development
          Initiative
OWG   Open Working Group
PPP   purchasing power parity
SDGs   Sustainable Development Goals
STEP   Society of Trust and Estate Practitioners
TBIJ   The Bureau of Investigative Journalism
TRACIT   Transnational Alliance to Combat Illicit
          Trade
UNCTAD   The UN Conference on Trade and
          Development
UNDP   United Nations Development Programme

UNICEF	United Nations Children's Fund
UNODC	UN Office for Drugs and Crime
VAT	value-added tax
WHO	World Health Organisation

Introduction

We may pride ourselves on being the generation of open data, of big data, of transparency and accountability, but the truth is less palatable. We are the generation of the uncounted – and we barely know it.

Imagine a world of such structural inequality that even the questions of who and what gets counted are decided by power. A world in which the 'unpeople' at the bottom go uncounted, as does the hidden 'unmoney' of those at the very top. Where the unpeople are denied a political voice and access to public services, while the unmoney escapes taxation, regulation and criminal investigation, allowing corruption and inequality to flourish out of sight.

This is the world we live in. A world of inequality, uncounted.

Actual and even perceived inequalities have large and wide-ranging, negative social impacts. Higher rates of child mortality, lower life expectancies, increased likelihood of conflict, reduced trust and social cohesion, increased corruption, lower economic growth and shorter growth cycles, on and on. When we accept higher inequality, we accept these inferior outcomes. We accept the absolute and certain waste of human potential that they impose.

We accept that women will work longer and for less income. We accept that indigenous populations and marginalized ethnolinguistic groups will be systematically excluded from educational opportunities and suffer poorer health. That people with disabilities will live poorer, shorter lives. As will people from marginalized geographic regions. And as for people at the intersections of one or more of these inequalities ...

Wait, though: we have broadly functional democracies, right? Surely it follows that those inequalities, those losses, are freely chosen by a majority. And if you don't like it, couldn't you just campaign for more people to care more about inequalities?

But debate over acceptable inequalities and acceptable redistributions is itself circumscribed by our failure to count. Political parties take positions on the basis of their ideological stance and their reading of popular concerns. Those positions mark out the space for mainstream political debate. And those positions, plus the underlying popular concerns, reflect in turn the data that is available and how it is presented.

What if common measures consistently understate the degree of income inequality, for example? Can the political debate still represent democratic preferences accurately? Or what if data is simply not collected on the inequalities facing certain groups: is the resulting absence of political debate legitimate? Or the absence of steps to reduce those groups' exclusion? What if the failure to count means that swathes of legal, regulatory and tax responsibilities do not fall equally on certain groups? And what if the very nature of our political processes is compromised, by a failure to count all votes or all voters equally, or to ensure that political funding is appropriately regulated, so that underlying economic inequalities can map themselves onto political outcomes?

The threat that this book addresses is that decisions seen as technical go unchallenged even though they are, in fact, powerfully political, creating a systematic bias towards levels of inequality that are needlessly high and do not reflect people's preferences. At the heart of the argument is the role played in society by statistics. I focus primarily on the analysis of data relating to the state, to which the term 'statistics' originally referred.

As a starting point, we can identify three core features of a state, and the related aspects of counting. First, take the state as a form of political representation. In whichever way it performs this 'who decides' function, it will reflect more or less well the views of citizens. This applies as much to the authoritarian state, which nonetheless requires some degree of popular support for its continuing legitimacy, as it does to the avowedly democratic state.

The state also performs a distributive role. For ease, I suggest a somewhat rough division between the second core feature, that of determining the distribution of benefits; and the third core feature, that of determining the distribution of responsibilities. There is inevitably overlap, and the split could be made elsewhere; but it is broadly useful to think of the categories as 'what people get' and 'what people are required to do'.

The distribution of benefits covers everything from the most direct to the least – from, say, levels of household transfers, regional investment decisions and the provision of public services and infrastructure, to the quality and resourcing of, for example, administrative and military functions. A state can perform this role more or less well, and more or less inclusively of the whole population.

The distribution of responsibilities covers the array of legal, judicial and regulatory functions, broadly defined, from the identification and policing of criminal behaviour, the design and enforcement of regulation and – crucially – of taxation. Again, a state can perform this role more or less well, and can ensure the application of regulation is more or less inclusive of the whole population.

Each of these three roles of the state depends on data. The questions of 'who decides', 'what people get' and 'what people are required to do' are answered in part by the underlying processes of counting. Political representation is determined by the counting of votes and of voters. The relative weighting of particular people and groups in the distributions of benefits, and of responsibilities, is determined by the counting of people for each purpose.

Crucially, the gathering of this data is far from unbiased (what Foucault terms 'governmentality'). Statistics and metrics do not simply appear fully formed, nor do they emerge from some neutral process of knowledge search, ready to be applied objectively to an optimal policy analysis. Instead, the interests of those who govern will be reflected in the very means of counting. Data is constructed in such a way as to support the emergence of social structures that are more 'governable'.

In Foucault's conception, this process *can* be a positive one:[1]

> We must cease once and for all to describe the effects of power in negative terms: it 'excludes', it 'represses', it 'censors', it 'abstracts', it 'masks', it 'conceals'. In fact, power produces; it produces reality; it produces domains of objects and rituals of truth. The individual and the knowledge that may be gained of him belong to this production.

The key point for our purposes is that the production of statistics and metrics, the process of *counting* that underpins state functions, is not abstract but deliberately willed. Most bluntly, this applies to the planning approaches that James C. Scott memorably dissects in *Seeing Like a State*:[2]

> The power and precision of high-modernist schemes depended not only on bracketing contingency but also on standardizing the subjects of development ... What is striking, of course, is that such subjects – like the 'unmarked citizens' of liberal theory – have, for the purposes of the planning exercise, no gender, no tastes, no history, no values, no opinions or original ideas, no traditions, and no distinctive personalities to contribute to the enterprise. They have none of the particular, situated, and contextual

attributes that one would expect of any population and that we, as a matter of course, always attribute to elites. The lack of context and particularity is not an oversight; it is the necessary first premise of any large-scale planning exercise.

The experience of the UN Millennium Development Goals (MDGs), discussed later, provides a good illustration of the point that being *blind* to the characteristics of people, households and groups does not result in neutral progress – quite the opposite. Recognizing the 'markings' of 'subjects', or refusing to do so, is likely to change significantly the processes of both planning and policy enactment.

Alain Desrosières identifies four attitudes of statisticians and others to the reality or otherwise of statistics.[3] The most obvious, which he labels 'metrological realism', rests on the assumption of some permanent reality, which is independent of any observation apparatus – so that quantitative social sciences could ultimately attain equivalent status to natural sciences.

In contrast, 'accounting realism' relates to a more limited space (internal to an enterprise or economic), but offers the illusory promise of rational, testable, provable numbers through double-entry bookkeeping. Illusory, because the numbers necessarily depend on a whole series of judgements – from those involved in the underlying business (or government of, say, a national economy), to the accountants involved directly in compiling the public record, and eventually to those behind the accounting frameworks in use.

The validity of this 'reality' depends in turn upon trust in those accountants and others – not in some objectively verifiable and unique set of data. If you're tempted to think accounting realism is anything but illusory, just ask anyone who has ever looked at the annual report of a multinational company to try to work out whether they paid the right tax, at the right time, in the right place.

Desrosières labels the third attitude 'proof in use'. Here, researchers using a given dataset prepared by some other body may evaluate its 'reality' on the basis of its internal consistency and/or of how well the *results* of their analysis conform with their priors. Good data with genuine inconsistencies may be undervalued, and institutions publishing statistics may have more incentive to ensure internal consistency of their data – even to the point of deliberately censoring genuine datapoints that do not conform with expectations. Finally, these three attitudes are contrasted with a fourth: one that recognizes explicitly 'that the definition and coding of the measured variables are "constructed", conventional, and arrived at through negotiation'.[4] There is no objective truth, but the constructed data can be more or less legitimate as a reflection of the different concerns and interests.

This point is extended in an important contribution by Wendy Espeland and Mitchell Stevens, which makes the case that 'quantification is fundamentally social – an artefact of human action, imagination, ambition, accomplishment, and failing'.[5] Measures not only reflect a view of people or things, but also lead people to change their behaviour – including policymakers, thereby creating the possibility of circular feedback between the (in any case overlapping) processes of government and measurement. That circularity is an inevitable feature, and can be both vicious and virtuous. In the case of the uncounted, poor data can promote poor policy, which in turn undermines the scope to improve data; but data improvements can also be self-reinforcing, driving a positive loop of better policy.

Specific metrics, above all where they allow ranking, can impose powerful (Foucaultian) discipline on the people and groups measured; that is, forms of accountability through transparency.[6] And so influence over the choice of metric, even for a fixed dataset, is an important form of power. Sakiko Fukuda-Parr and others examined a wide range of metrics selected in the context of the UN Sustainable Development Goals (SDGs), illustrating exactly how competing actors have sought (and achieved) political influence over supposedly technical processes and decisions.[7]

The choice of who and what go *un*counted, excluded either from the gathered statistics or from the chosen metrics, is equally a question of power. And the roles of power and social construction in counting are not optional. There is no 'neutral' option in which counting decisions are taken in a vacuum, free from political concerns. And there are no meaningful counting decisions that do not have political implications.

We cannot design a system that inoculates societies from these core characteristics of counting. But we can inoculate ourselves to a degree, from the 'seduction of quantification', by opening our eyes to it: by understanding the central dynamics, and the possible nature and extent of the biases that result. We can count better. And if we do, the world can *be* better.

In this book, I look at a range of important counting choices as they are actually made. I consider the implications for inequality, for governance and for human progress. I use the term 'uncounted' to describe a politically motivated failure to count. This takes two main forms, and each has direct implications for inequalities.

First, there may be people and groups at the bottom of distributions (e.g., income) whose 'uncounting' adds another level to their marginalization – for example, where they are absent from statistics that underpin political representation ('who decides') and also inform policy prioritization ('what people get'). Second, there may be people and groups at the top of distributions who are further empowered by being able to go uncounted – not least by hiding income and wealth from taxation and regulation ('what people are required to do'). The uncounted at the bottom are excluded; the uncounted at the top are escaping.

A further distinction in each case lies between what we can call 'relative' and 'absolute' uncounting. In the former, people or groups are included within the data sample, but are not differentiated. For example, household surveys may include (some) transgender people but without differentiation will fail to generate comparative data on how this group fares. Or consolidated company accounts may reveal information about a multinational's global profits and tax, but without revealing the relative positions of its operations in Luxembourg, say, or Kenya. Absolute uncounting, meanwhile, reflects the complete failure to include a group – whether that be the absence of high net-worth tax evaders from wealth distribution data, or of some rural, indigenous populations from census data.

Questions of power being complex, there are also cases when marginalized groups may seek to be uncounted precisely in order to exert some power. Any desire to be counted in order to provide a basis for curtailing inequalities will be remote, when the purpose of a state's counting is to impose greater inequalities.[8] Think of oppressed populations fighting to avoid being singled out – whether against the use of the Star of David to isolate Jews in Nazi Germany, for example, or against the use of 'pass books' as tools of racial discrimination in South Africa, from the eighteenth century up until the apartheid regime; or the resistance in certain cases to group identification in census surveys (the 'I'm Spartacus' response).[9]

Hidden identity through collective pseudonyms has a long history as a tool of resistance also. Marco Deseriis tracks the use of 'improper names' in groups from the Luddites of the nineteenth century, to the modern-day Luther Blissett Project and the Anonymous hacker collective, and argues that they share three features:[10]

1 Empowering a subaltern social group by providing a medium for identification and mutual recognition to their users.
2 Enabling those who do not have a voice of their own to acquire a symbolic power outside the boundaries of an institutional practice.

3 Expressing a process of subjectivation characterized by the proliferation of difference.

Depending on the external conditions – the power faced, and its legitimacy to count or identify – the case for being uncounted, and the space to do so, will vary. There is a clear difference, however, between the 'guerrilla' tactics of the relatively powerless seeking to go uncounted in the face of a quantifying bureaucracy, and the exertion of power by those at the top to escape or circumvent counting.

Inevitably, counting at the national level is imperfect. Survey and census data tend to have major flaws, as does the administrative data used for taxation and voting – and yet these are the basis for any number of crucial policy decisions about where and how to allocate resources.

If the missing data were more or less random, any overall distortions would be limited. If, on the other hand, there were systematic patterns to the distortions, then we should be less sanguine. And, of course, it turns out that what goes uncounted is not random after all.

Instead, the failure to count is directly related to the power of those involved. At the bottom, those who are excluded tend to be from already marginalized groups. The established weaknesses of these data include the almost universal absence of good statistics on lesbian, gay, bisexual and transgender (LGBT) populations and persons living with disabilities, as well as country-specific failures around indigenous populations and racial and ethnolinguistic groups. And the absence of good statistics can lead, in turn, to the absence of a profile for these groups in public policy discussions and prioritization decisions.

Sometimes, supporters of the status quo will use the fact of a phenomenon being uncounted as an argument against addressing the underlying inequalities. The fight for international tax justice, for example, has seen a number of phases. First, policymakers would deny that tax avoidance and tax evasion were a significant problem. Then, when presented with estimates of substantial scale, the response would often be that the big numbers are not sufficiently robust. Only under the pressure that stems from media coverage and public awareness of those big numbers have international institutions themselves begun to estimate the scale of the problem – often coming up with bigger numbers than had campaigners, and finally leading to sustained policy engagement.

There is important value to the process of testing and probing estimates, both to improve their quality and as part of the social legitimation of their construction. But this can also often provide cover for defenders of the status quo simply to raise doubts about the validity of the underlying concerns. In the tax justice space, this is typically expressed as the view that the big numbers are not robust, so there is no 'pot of gold' to be had from stopping multinationals' tax avoidance. It is clearer now, when that view continues to be expressed despite a range of new data sources and research by independent academics and from international institutions, that much of the support for it is politically rather than technically motivated. But in the early stages of the tax justice movement, there was a genuine risk that the absence of better data could have provided the defenders of the status quo with a conclusive argument against progress.

Bad statistics used to advocate for change can be exploited by what we might call the 'uncounted lobby'. A paradigmatic example has been the claim made that the informal settlements in Kibera, Nairobi, constitute 'Africa's largest slum'. Over time, the challenges to this deeply flawed statistical claim have contributed both to improve the true understanding of the area and its development challenges, and to raise the standard to which development nongovernmental organizations (NGOs) hold themselves in respect of similar claims. But at the same time, the absence of good data backing this particular claim has provided fodder to those with a broader political agenda to downplay concerns about global poverty, and to attack NGOs and others arguing for justice.[11] The claim was comprehensively debunked by Kenya's census, and covered with high profile in the *Daily Nation* newspaper as the results were released in 2010. But two years later, international reporting was claiming credit for applying their scepticism to 'Africa's propaganda trail' – a much wider claim that seemed intent on undermining a whole sector.

Or consider the 'zombie stats' around women's inequality: in particular, the claims that women make up 70 per cent of the world's (extreme income) poor, and that women own only 1 per cent of the world's land.[12] For the uncounted lobby, the fact that neither of these can be stood up by available data is evidence that supporters of women's equality are misguided, extreme, talking about a problem that doesn't exist, etc. For the rest of us, the fact that we (still) don't have the data to know how extreme the income and wealth inequalities facing women are, is itself an obvious part of the problem.

Being counted does not guarantee that inequalities will be addressed. But being uncounted certainly makes inequalities less visible, and progress less likely. James Baldwin put it better: 'Not everything that is faced can be changed, but nothing can be changed until it is faced.'[13]

At the top, inequality is hidden in three main ways. First, inequality is hidden through missing data: while the poorest groups are underrepresented in surveys, high-income households are much less likely to respond to surveys and are therefore omitted. This can be fixed by using data from tax authorities, where available, which has been seen to add significantly to observed inequality.

Second, and most blatantly, there is deliberate hiding of income and assets by those with most power. This means that the tax data itself contains important omissions. Through the use of anonymous companies and the exploitation of bank secrecy, substantial sums of wealth and the resulting income streams are hidden overseas by high-income households all around the world. Thomas Piketty, in his landmark study *Capital in the Twenty-First*

Century, suggested that an estimate of the volume of undeclared assets of around 10 per cent of global gross domestic
product (GDP) should be thought of as the lowest possible
level. This is part of Piketty's reasoning for a global wealth
tax – that, actual revenue and redistributive effects aside,
such a policy would ensure that the distribution data at
least exist.

Multinational companies use similar secrecy mecha-
nisms, coupled with accounting opacity, to shift massive
volumes of profits out of the tax jurisdictions where they
arise. Together, individual and corporate tax abuses
drain hundreds of billions of dollars in revenue from governments around the world each year, undermining the
effectiveness of progressive, direct taxation – and broader
attempts to hold accountable these largest of the world's
economic actors.

The third way in which income inequality goes
uncounted is more subtle, but perhaps equally poisonous.
The Gini coefficient, the default measure for inequality, is
inherently flawed – and in such a way that it is relatively
insensitive to the tails of the distribution (the parts we care
about most), and increasingly insensitive at higher levels
of inequality (the times when we care most). So what is
presented as a neutral, technical measure in fact imparts
a serious bias to our understanding of inequality and its
development over time. Overall, we know much less about
inequality of wealth and income at the top than we do for
most of the distribution – and the most common inequality
measure exacerbates this problem still further. Metrics, as
well as statistics, are distorted by power and in turn distort
political outcomes.

Similar problems play out in the area of what we might
call 'privately counted' data. These include cases where
data of significant public value is indeed gathered but is
held by private companies with an interest in what part of it
is publicly countable, and how. The roles of Facebook and
Cambridge Analytica in the UK's Brexit referendum and
the election of Donald Trump as US President highlight the

potential threat to democracy.[14] Another example is that of the limitations of access to medical trial data generated by pharmaceutical companies. Ben Goldacre has shown how the failure to regulate for effective access to medical trial data results in inferior medical treatments continuing to be widely marketed and used – with human impacts up to and including large-scale excess mortality.[15]

Cathy O'Neil's analysis of the biases in algorithms reveals just how far we are from the dream that big data or its use in the public or private sectors could be a tool for equalizing power. Instead, there are multiple, opaque avenues for discrimination, both deliberate and accidental, with grave implications for a range of inequalities.[16] More trivially, unless you take seriously Bill Shankly's suggestion that football surpasses life and death in importance, the Tax Justice Network's *Offshore Game* project has shown how the unregulated financial secrecy used by owners can lead football fans to suffer all sorts of risks – including exploitation and even liquidation of their clubs.[17]

The common thread across all the cases touched on here is the relationship between power, inequality and being uncounted – a relationship that demands we pay much more attention to who and what are and are not counted. The sociologist William Bruce Cameron observed that not everything that can be counted counts, and not everything that counts can be counted.[18] While this antimetabole is undoubtedly true, so, too, is another: much that goes uncounted matters, and much that matters goes uncounted.

There are reasons to be optimistic: as attention to inequality has grown, so, too, has awareness of the need to reveal the uncounted. Concerted efforts to challenge the uncounted at the bottom and the top are possible now in a way that simply was not the case even ten years ago.

The first part of this book explores the uncounted at the bottom of the distribution, ranging from international development findings to evidence of the exclusion of marginalized groups in high-income countries. The second part focuses on the uncounted at the top of the distribution.

This includes the core tax justice analysis of the nature and extent of financial secrecy, the scale of revenue losses through 'tax havens' promoting individual tax evasion and multinational profit shifting, as well as the largely unacknowledged bias that overreliance on the Gini coefficient introduces into common perceptions of inequality. Together, the evidence points towards great damage being done to the world's prospects for genuinely sustainable human progress – and quite unnecessarily.

The book concludes with an Uncounted Manifesto: a political and technical call to action, to change the relationships we tolerate between data, power and inequality. Before they change us any further ...

Our societies owe a debt to those we have caused to go uncounted, through their marginalization. At the same time, we are owed a debt by those who conspire to hide from tax and other responsibilities. Both debts are rising by the day, and both are driving up inequality, uncounted. Before we can make the past right, we must stop the clock. We need to understand the systematic flaws that make us ignorant of ourselves and our world – and start counting as if we cared.

Part I

Uncounted and Excluded: The Unpeople Hidden at the Bottom

As we embark on this great collective journey, we pledge that no one will be left behind.

Recognizing that the dignity of the human person is fundamental, we wish to see the Goals and targets met for all nations and peoples and for all segments of society. And we will endeavour to reach the furthest behind first.

UN Sustainable Development Goals[1]

Would it not be a great satisfaction for the King to know every year in precise terms the number of his subjects, in full and in detail, including all the personal effects, riches and poverty of each house; that of the nobility of the sword and of the clerics of all kinds, of the nobility of the robe, of Catholics and members of other religions, each individual with the places they inhabit? Would it not be a great pleasure, but also a useful and necessary pleasure, to be able himself and from his cabinet to cover in an hour the present and the past of a great kingdom of which he is the chief, and to be able to know by himself and with certainty its greatness, its riches and its strength? This could be done in an orderly fashion, in full and in detail, by means of well-drawn maps, both general and particular, that could be added to the tables of counting which, repeated once every year, would show him precisely and clearly his gains and his losses, the increase or decline of his Estate, the increase or decrease of his peoples, and that of the livestock which are the foundation of men's subsistence and of trade. And the comparison of the old counts with the new would enable him to judge soundly the changes occurring in the provinces ...

Marquis de Vauban, proposing an annual census
to Louis XIV of France in 1686[2]

1

Development's Data Problem

What we measure affects what we do; and if our measurements are flawed, decisions may be distorted ... [I]f our metrics of performance are flawed, so too may be the inferences that we draw.

The Stiglitz–Sen–Fitoussi Report (2009)[1]

This chapter summarizes several decades of shifts in development thinking and the associated indicators, from GDP to UN development goals. Those indicators have great power – including the power to embed massive biases in development policy and in the progress made.

Everyone knows that development has a data problem. However, different people understand that statement to mean quite different things. For some, 'development' is the study of poor countries, and the data problem is that those countries aren't good enough at generating the data needed to study them. For others, 'development' is the process by which poor countries and poor people stop being so poor, and the data problem is about having the information to improve that process.

But these ideas of development are themselves problematic: the notion that some countries (or people) have developed, or are developed; while others are develop*ing*, or yet to develop. Increasingly, we think of 'development' as shorthand for the whole subject of how human beings live on this planet, the ways in which we as a species organize ourselves from the local to the global, to provide the greatest opportunities for each person in current and future generations to live a good life.

A good life might be considered as one in which people have a degree of power in various spheres: the personal (in which empowerment implies that people enjoy a level of health, education and mental well-being, along with decent work and leisure conditions); the economic (a broadly secure level of income, and freedom from extreme inequality); the political (political freedom and political security, i.e. freedom from political violence or instability); and the social (community well-being, social relations and environmental conditions including environmental security, i.e. freedom from environmental fluctuations).[2] On this view, poverty is a lack of power – and so is fundamentally political, rather than (say) strictly financial, and necessarily complex and multifaceted.

The data problem for development, understood in these terms, is grave. Typically, we lack sufficient data in countries at all levels of per capita income to ensure that these aspects of a decent life are met. Moreover, the weaknesses of data are not consistent but discriminatory. The data to determine political representation ('who decides') and to inform policy prioritization ('what people get') tends, as we will see, to exclude further precisely the people and groups who are already marginalized. Development's data problem reflects a mixture of genuine absences of quantification, deliberate manipulation and bias – in both the collection and the use of data. Those weaknesses, together, are consistently disempowering of marginalized people and groups – effectively deepening their experiences of poverty and inequalities.

Counting is crucial to understanding development. But if we seek to understand development only by what is *already* counted, we lock in the underlying inequalities. This is to make the same mistake as the drunk who searches for their keys under the lamppost despite having dropped them at the dark end of the street, simply because it is the only place they can see. The emergence and maintenance of effective states, and their capacity to promote and support human progress, depend upon the numbers available and selected. At the same time, differences in development thought have implications for the type of counting that is prioritized, and therefore for the numbers that are available.

If the history of development thought is simplified to a series of evolutionary steps in counting, then in each stage we see that mainstream aims have become more nuanced and more relevant to the lived experience of populations. Inevitably, this greater nuance has driven better counting (that is, better measurement of a population's lived experience). However, the causality runs in both directions because at the same time, better measurement has revealed important realities that have in turn informed different mainstream priorities.

'Development' has itself developed, from the longstanding preoccupation in which economic growth, or the rate of increase in countries' GDP, was the dominant metric of success. The Commission on the Measurement of Economic Performance and Social Progress (the 'Stiglitz–Sen–Fitoussi Report' quoted above) was primarily focused on rejecting GDP as a meaningful metric of progress, but GDP remains disproportionately salient, along with the simple average of economic activity per person, GDP per capita, as a basis to track and compare countries' development.

GDP: Global Data Problem

GDP poses problems both because of what it does not aim to count, and because of how it fails to count even on its own terms. The most egregious issues, in terms of what GDP does not aim to count, are two. One is the absence of any reflection at all that economic output may come at a planetary cost. If activity is less than totally sustainable, pursuing increases in a measure of total activity may prove to be the ultimate in pyrrhic victories – quite literally. The other is the failure to count unpaid activities – in general, and in particular. In general, because if only what's counted counts, then the dominance of GDP must bear some responsibility for the trend of which it forms a part, towards narrow economic evaluation, and the devaluing of other human outputs including cultural public goods. And in particular, because GDP is a gender-biased measure of a reality that is itself already deeply, structurally unequal.[3]

Women's participation in the labour force globally is estimated to be 26 percentage points lower than that of men. Women also earn less for their participation: 24 per cent less on average, globally. These facts alone would mean that GDP reflects a disproportionately male scale of economic activity – even on top of the inequalities that give rise to the facts in the first place. But it is the additional features of women's economic oppression that make GDP especially, almost perfectly biased as a single measure of 'progress'.

Women's participation in the labour force occurs disproportionately in a sector that is largely or completely excluded from GDP statistics: subsistence agriculture. We might think there is a pretty sizeable economic value, not to mention a human one, to people subsisting rather than not – but if there is, GDP does not count it. Finally, of course, women also contribute disproportionately to unpaid care. According to UN Women, the source of all these statistics, 'in all regions women work more than men: on average they do almost two and a half times as much unpaid care and domestic work as men, and if paid and unpaid work are combined, women in almost all countries work longer hours than men each day'.[4] Time-use surveys suggest that the economic value of unpaid care and domestic work ranges widely across countries, between around 10 per cent and 40 per cent of GDP; the one constant is the great majority being undertaken by women and girls.

The effect of GDP would stop at adding statistical insult to development injury were it not for the absolute dominance of GDP as to what remains *the* most important indicator of national progress. Angela Davis has emphasized the case that Marxist scholar Walter Rodney makes in *How Europe Underdeveloped Africa*, that one legacy of colonial occupation was the distinction imposed between men's work as 'modern', while women's work was 'traditional' and 'backward'. This is a legacy that the power of GDP has arguably maintained to this day.[5] The invisibilization by GDP of women's contribution to society may be the gravest single example of the phenomenon of the uncounted.

Imagine visitors from another planet arriving to discover that a small majority of the dominant species on Earth are systematically excluded from the main 'progress' measure. If our visitors were to set aside for a moment the outright foolishness of largely ignoring the planetary costs of our economic activity, they would perceive rightly that on the basis of GDP, humanity is likely to pursue 'growth' characterized by a systematic neglect of policies that could rapidly increase progress if only women's contribution were to be more fully counted.

The measure also means that policymakers are likely to see 'formalization' as the answer – moving women's activity into the bit that's counted, rather than improving how we count the other bits. Formalization is not necessarily bad, but it is the most narrow response possible. If you rule out all others without thinking about it, the measure has decided policy for you. Such an approach risks becoming a form of statistical victim-blaming, in which the fault lies with women's failure to participate in formal employment rather than in GDP's failure to count their contributions, which in turn hides governments' failures to address the systemic roots of inequality.

Our visitors might go further still, and realize that the

economic activity of some other groups, including most notably certain indigenous populations, is also systematically likely to be uncounted by GDP. Coupled with the failure to recognize an economic value to sustainability, this exacerbates the tendency towards policies that destroy uncounted habitats and unvalued ways of life in the name of economic progress. Where these groups intersect with gender, the problems stemming from ill-measurement are likely to be deepest.

The use of GDP per capita as a more human-centred measure is no less problematic in this regard. Because it is blind to the actual distribution of GDP (if we even consider a per person distribution of GDP to be conceptually meaningful), the impulse is again towards increasing GDP rather than any actual improvement in people's lived experience – say, by reducing inequalities.

In terms of what GDP *does* set out to measure, the data are subject to widespread failure by countries to generate quality series. The failings of lower-income countries, however, have been much more widely condemned than those of higher-income counterparts. For lower-income countries, the weaknesses stem most often from a failure to commit resources to regular rebasing. This can mean that as the shape of an economy changes – for example, with agriculture becoming proportionately smaller as manufacturing or services grow – the estimation of GDP relies on increasingly outdated basic data, and so becomes increasingly inaccurate.

The World Bank's Shanta Devarajan wrote of Africa's 'statistical tragedy' in 2011, and in 2013 Bill Gates named economic historian Morten Jerven's *Poor Numbers: How We Are Misled by African Development Statistics and What To Do About It* one of his books of the year.[6] Devarajan highlights the case of Ghana, which a year earlier had revised the basis for its series resulting in a 62 per cent increase in recorded GDP, in the process passing per capita GDP of $1,000 and so being reclassified by the World Bank from low- to middle-income country status.

This illustrates the potential for countries to benefit from rebasing decisions, where delay may mean retaining access to subsidized international funding – a view supported to a degree by subsequent research.[7]

On the flip side, rebasing to show (true) GDP growth can contribute to a narrative of economic success that policymakers may believe likely to be self-reinforcing. There is also evidence of outright manipulation of GDP series for political purposes. A study from the University of Chicago uses data on nighttime light emissions, as captured by satellites, to evaluate the accuracy of public GDP series, and claims to find that the most authoritarian regimes inflate their GDP by a factor of 1.15 to 1.3.[8] For both types of reason, the timing of rebasing may provide a small degree of power to lower-income countries; but exerting that power may come at the cost of statistical quality.

While the resulting statistical weaknesses are largely recognized, there is rather less agreement (not least among African statisticians, who may be considered to have relevant expertise and valid perspectives) with the idea that the quality of GDP data should take an even higher priority over other development data, given the limited resources available. Pali Lehohla, then Statistician General of South Africa and Chairman of the Statistical Commission of Africa, agreed on the importance of rebasing GDP series on a regular basis, but responded angrily to Morten Jerven's book. Lehohla argued that the analysis did not reflect the depth of statistical expertise on the continent, nor the progress that had been made, and risked distorting regional priorities.

Much less profile is given to the weaknesses and manipulation of GDP series in high-income countries, even though the evidence is much more direct. An interesting finding of the University of Chicago study is that after adjusting for authoritarian manipulation, the country with the fastest growing GDP from 1992/3 to 2005/6 was Ireland. But Ireland's GDP is perhaps the most overtly distorted of any economy of significant size, because of its role as one of the most significant tax havens for corporate profit shifting. For example, staff at the International Monetary Fund (IMF) estimate that in 2017, a quarter of Ireland's economic growth came from exports of Apple iPhones – even though Ireland does not actually export any iPhones at all.[9]

The quality of Ireland's GDP statistics has been sacrificed for years at the altar of tax havenry. The artificial recording of economic activity that actually takes place elsewhere (and/or the resulting taxable income) is, however, a mere footnote in relation to the revenue losses imposed on those other countries – or the divergence between actual Irish household incomes and per capita GDP. Similarly, the UK Crown Dependency of Jersey, with a population around 100,000, had for some years in the 2000s what was estimated as the highest per capita income in the world, even while foodbanks operated on the island (and continue to do so) for those struggling to subsist.

We consider the statistical distortions flowing from 'tax haven' behaviours in Part II, but present this as a cautionary tale for now. Narratives matter, and the narrative of bad data as one more problem of lower-income countries has unfortunately gained much more traction than the counternarrative that data from all countries should be critically understood as reflecting a range of issues of power and incentives. In the European Union (EU), for example, Greece is widely seen since the financial crisis of 2008 as having manipulated national economic data to get round EU budgetary rules. (Extraordinarily, the former president of the Greek statistics office, Andreas Georgiou, was in 2018 given a two-year suspended prison sentence for having had the temerity in 2009 to insist on publishing accurate deficit statistics – specifically, of 15.4 per cent of GDP rather than 13.6 per cent of GDP – reversing manipulations that had run in varying ways and degrees since 1997, but also, according to some, precipitating the imposition of austerity. The revisions that Georgiou insisted upon were to bring the data in line with the European standard ESA95, and the approach continues to be used today.)[10] Research also shows that the same manipulations appeared across the EU membership, so that Greece was not a *special* case but merely a more extreme case, in line with the observed pattern.[11]

The continuing, absolute dominance of GDP should be treated as a political issue of the utmost seriousness, rather than as a mere technical puzzle. Few of those engaged with the actual statistics or their creation are blind to its weaknesses. But partial scepticism does not protect against the gradual pull of bad data. That pull takes us towards economic progress that continues to exclude the un(der) counted, notably women and indigenous populations. It also detracts from meaningful efforts to ensure human progress is ecologically sustainable. And it ignores, by and large, the serious quality issues – especially those relating to higher-income countries.

As an indicator of our global data problems, GDP is hard to beat.

Developing Thought

It is three decades since the first major, institutional crack became visible in the dominance of GDP. In the time since, both development thought and the associated counting have seen substantial shifts. GDP may not have been displaced, but the landscape of complementary and alternative measures is very different.

The crucial interventions came from the UN Children's Fund's (UNICEF) *Adjustment with a Human Face* (1987) and the UN Development Programme's (UNDP) first Human Development Report (1990), which made the case respectively for focusing on poor people rather than on poor countries, and for non-GDP aspects of national progress.[12] The more conservative World Bank promoted extreme income poverty as the central element, from the subsequent 1990 World Development Report. This approach gave rise to the 'dollar-a-day' measure, with its manifold and deep flaws. But even this represented an important progression from GDP-based measures, with their complete blindness to questions of distribution.

The World Bank's 'dollar-a-day' measure was eventually adopted as the basis for the target of the first UN Millennium Development Goal in 2000. The Millennium Development Goals (MDGs) together represented the first attempt to establish a common set of progress measures, albeit for lower-income countries only. Alongside, and partly in response to, the primary focus on absolute, monetary poverty came a much wider and richer analysis of individual and household poverty, more closely reflecting the UNICEF and UNDP contributions. There were eight goals, each with a range of indicators to track progress:

Goal 1 Eradicate extreme poverty and hunger
Goal 2 Achieve universal primary education
Goal 3 Promote gender equality and empower women
Goal 4 Reduce child mortality
Goal 5 Improve maternal health
Goal 6 Combat HIV/AIDS, malaria and other diseases
Goal 7 Ensure environmental sustainability
Goal 8 Develop a global partnership for development

The MDGs provide a partial reflection of a major shift in the underlying analysis. Three approaches going beyond monetary poverty measures can be identified.[13] First, the capabilities approach follows Amartya Sen's influential work and treats poverty as the failure to achieve certain minimal capabilities – rather than as the failure to reach a certain consumption or income level.[14] While the emphasis remains on absolute achievements, the capabilities approach is necessarily a multidimensional one, going far beyond income as a proxy for utility.

The social exclusion approach emphasizes the *relative* rather than the *absolute* aspects of poverty, and hence the ability of people to participate in a given society. Lacking internet access when everyone else has it, for example, may have different implications from the case where no one has access. From this approach tends to follow an understanding of poverty as clearly multidimensional, and significant attention to group characteristics (since these are frequently the basis for exclusion). The relative approach supports a greater emphasis on inequalities.

Finally, the participatory approach seeks to elicit views from within communities on the nature and locus of poverty. Important concerns here reflect issues around doing this without introducing external bias and ensuring the views that are heard are genuinely representative (a problem that looms ever larger as attempts are made to take this approach to national scale). There are also inherent problems of self-identification (including, for example, the tendency to identify others as [more] poor [than oneself]).

Table 1 builds on Ruggeri-Laderchi et al.'s comparison of these approaches with that of monetary poverty, and this is where the MDGs can reasonably be situated. Rather than specify a single definition or approach, and despite giving the World Bank's income poverty measure the headline focus, the framework as a whole set in place a breadth of goals and targets that owed much more to the capabilities approach. In both aspects, the MDGs marked a final break from seeing development as a problem of 'poor countries', and focused instead on poor people.

Bad Incentives, Bad Data

As the economist Sakiko Fukuda-Parr wrote, the MDGs were 'used in two ways as an instrument of global governance. The first is as a norm, to create incentives that lead to behaviour change. The second is to describe social objectives in concrete terms and communicate them.'[15] While this makes the indicators for a framework of targets like the MDGs potentially powerful norm-setters, data are

Table 1: A comparison of four approaches to poverty

	Monetary poverty	Capability approach	Social exclusion approach	Participatory approach
Importance in MDGs	High profile, although central only to MDG 1.	Substantial.	Minimal.	Negligible.
Unit of analysis	Ideally the individual, de facto the household.	The individual.	Individuals or groups relative to others in their community and/or society.	Groups, and individuals within them.
Interpreted by policymakers as requiring:	Emphasis on economic growth and distribution of monetary income.	Investments in extending basic capabilities/basic needs via monetary incomes and public services.	Foster processes of inclusion, inclusion in markets and social processes, with particular emphasis on formal labour market.	Empowerment of the poor.
Data availability (as at 2003)	Household surveys regularly conducted; omitted observations can be important. Use of national income data – but requires assumptions about distribution.	Data less regularly collected, but could easily be improved.	Currently have to rely on data collected for other purposes. If agreed on basic dimensions, data could be regularly collected.	Generally only small purposive samples. Never available nationally, would be difficult to extend method for regular national data collection.

Major weaknesses for measurement	Needs to be anchored to external elements. Arbitrary.	Impossibility of set evaluation. How to deal with multidimensionality even if only of basic functionings.	Problems with multidimensionality. Challenge of capturing process.	How comparable? How representative?
Required or minimum standard identified by:	Reference to 'external' information (defined outside the unit); central element food requirements.	Reference to 'lists' of dimensions normally assumed to be objectively definable.	Reference to those prevailing in society and state. Obligations.	Local people's own perceptions of well-being and ill-being.
Major weaknesses conceptually	Utility is not an adequate measure of well-being, and poverty is not an economic category.	Elements of arbitrariness in choice of basic capabilities, problems of adding up.	Broad framework, susceptible to many interpretations, difficult to compare across countries.	Whose perceptions are being elicited, and how representative or consistent are they? How does one deal with disagreements?
Problems for cross-country comparisons	Comparability of surveys, of price indices, of drawing poverty lines.	Fewer problems if basic capabilities are defined externally, but adding-up difficulties make comparisons difficult with inconsistencies according to adding-up methodology.	Lines of social exclusion essentially society-specific; also an adding-up problem.	Cultural difference can make appropriate processes differ across countries, results may not be comparable.

Source: Adapted from Caterina Ruggeri-Laderchi, Ruhi Saith and Frances Stewart, 2003, 'Does it matter that we do not agree on the definition of poverty? A comparison of four approaches', *Oxford Development Studies* 31(3), table 3.

inevitably problematic when made, by policy, the subject of direct conflicts of interest.

Goodhart's Law is named after Charles Goodhart, who, in considering monetary targeting for a central bank, wrote: 'Any observed statistical regularity will tend to collapse once pressure is placed upon it for control purposes.'[16] Development is rife with confirmatory examples.

An important report on development data from the end of the MDG period explores two obvious cases.[17] First, the authors look at the divergence (in Kenya and Tanzania) between school enrolment as measured by household survey data (that is, what people themselves report) and that measured by administrative data (as reported by the relevant institutions). A systematic element of the divergence can be explained by schools having public funding streams that depend on the reported numbers of pupils. In other words, where institutions have a financial interest in the data they report, that data will become unreliable. In countries where this is the case, the data tracking MDG progress on education enrolment will be consistently biased.

A second, parallel example comes from statistics on vaccinations. Where the Global Alliance on Vaccinations and Immunizations (GAVI) began offering low-income countries a financial incentive for each child receiving the third dose of the vaccine against diphtheria, tetanus, and pertussis (DTP3), based on administrative data, that series diverged from the reporting in household surveys. That is, because countries (or their institutions) had a financial interest in the data they themselves reported, the data became unreliable. The equivalent series for measles immunization, where no such financial incentive was in place, showed no change over the period. Again, the reporting of key data on progress was predictably distorted.

At the international level, the incentives to distort are equally present. Perhaps the most blatant political, rather than financial, manipulation can be found in the MDGs themselves. The emblematic success story for many has been MDG 1. Or, rather, MDG target 1(a), which oddly is not the eradication but the halving of world poverty. Over and above that sleight of hand, a closer look at the counting that underlines this claim shows it to be even more problematic.

Criticism of MDG 1 has focused on three main aspects. The substantive question has been whether it is valuable, or reasonable, to target the number of people living in extreme income poverty (on $1 a day, or $1.90 as it is now after some allowance for inflation) – as opposed to more ambitious income measures, or indicators of multidimensional human development gains. This is perhaps most simply seen in the fact that the 'dollar-a-day' measure was intended to capture some level of being able to meet basic human needs, from an amalgamation of national poverty lines. But while the extreme income poverty headcount fell from around 1.9 billion people in 1990, to under 750 million in 2015, the number of those deemed to be undernourished – i.e., without the income to avoid the most basic effects of extreme income poverty – is estimated to stand at around 1.5 billion people.[18] In other words, the dollar-a-day measure correlates very poorly indeed with what it was intended to capture: the ability to meet the most basic human needs.

Second, there continues to be fierce technical debate over whether the World Bank's numbers do actually provide a meaningful tracking of extreme income poverty in any particular case. Here the criticisms reflect in part the weaknesses of the underlying data, including major gaps for countries and regions, and other cases that appear to be based on extrapolation from other countries. More detailed critiques relate to the use of artificial exchange rates adjusted between countries for 'purchasing power parity' (PPP); of the appropriate inflation measures at national level but also to address price variations within countries (especially rural–urban differentials, but also the scope for lower-income households to face different pricing regardless of location); and of the appropriateness of combining income and consumption data.

The potential importance of group-appropriate inflation rates can be seen in a study by the Joseph Rowntree
Foundation on UK poverty.[19] The authors find that
between 2002–3 and 2013–14, an official inflation rate of
3.1 per cent hid an annual average inflation rate of 3.4 per
cent for the bottom quintile of households, compared with
3 per cent for the top quintile. In all but one year studied,
the inflation rate was higher for the poorest quintile. While
the differential may sound small, it adds up: the real cost
of living was shown to rise 50 per cent for low-income
households, compared with 43 per cent for high-income
households, with the result that the UK's absolute income
poverty was 0.5 percentage points higher at the end of
the period than the standard measures suggest: an extra
300,000 people in poverty, uncounted.

Returning to global poverty, the impact of individual technical decisions on the outcome statistics is also
great. Sanjay Reddy and Rahul Lahoti of the Global
Consumption and Income Project show, for example, that
the World Bank decision to consider different rural and
urban PPP conversions in three large countries (China,
India and Indonesia), may have affected the 2011 global
extreme income poverty headcount by some 290 million.[20]
They add, tellingly: 'The Bank has offered no sensitivity
analysis nor discussed the impact of this choice, leaving
open the question of why it made the particular decisions
that it did.'

The third critique of MDG 1, and the claims of success,
is a more basic one: that the goalposts were moved.[21] As
Table 2 shows, the implication of those movements was
dramatic for the number of people whom the world effectively agreed to tolerate living in extreme income poverty.
The 1996 World Food Summit (the 'Rome Declaration')
sought to halve the (1996) numbers in poverty worldwide,
implying a final 'acceptable' level by 2015 of 850 million
people. The Millennium Declaration of 2000 backdated
the start point to 1990 (to include a relatively successful
decade), and sought to halve the *proportion* of people in

Table 2: Shifting the goalposts on global poverty reduction commitments

	World Food Summit	MDG 1 as adopted	MDG 1, revised
Language of target	Halve the world's number of undernourished people; 'Poverty is a major cause of food insecurity and sustainable progress in poverty eradication is critical.'	Halve the proportion of the world's people in extreme income poverty, and of those suffering hunger.	Halve the proportion of the developing world population in extreme income poverty, and of those suffering hunger.
Reference year	1996	2000	1990
Reference population	5.80 billion	6.12 billion	4.25 billion
Proportion in extreme income poverty	29.40%	27.60%	44.50%
Target population	1.70 billion	1.69 billion	1.89 billion
2015 reference population	7.36 billion	7.36 billion	7.29 billion
2015 target population	0.85 billion	1.02 billion	1.36 billion
2015 target as proportion of world population	11.6%	13.8%	18.5%

Note: Data for world and 'developing country' (low- and middle-income country) population and extreme income poverty headcount ratios are taken from the World Bank. Proportions in extreme income poverty in 2000 are linear extrapolations (for 'developing countries', 1999: 34.8%, 2002: 31%; and world, 1999: 28.0%, 2002: 25.6%).

poverty – a smaller reach given that population growth made the original target more ambitious. The effect was to raise the 'acceptable' 2015 level above a billion people.

Finally, and most dramatically, the revised MDG 1 target switched the base from the proportion of world population in poverty to the proportion of people in low- and middle-income countries. This seemingly innocuous rewording had a major effect, raising the implicitly acceptable level of 2015 poverty to 1.36 billion people: half a billion more than the 1996 target.

Now, at least on the basis of the World Bank's count, each of the three versions of the target was comfortably met. But put this in context: had the World Bank not made different choices for three countries about rural–urban pricing patterns, the variance identified by Reddy and Lahoti, of 290 million additional people in poverty, would result in both the Rome Declaration and Millennium Declaration targets having been missed.

The opacity of those decisions means that we can't know for sure if the World Bank got them 'right', or those for other countries where the decision went the other way. But we can know for sure that success in meeting the global target to reduce extreme income poverty, except in the least ambitious, final watering-down, was dependent on those decisions.

The institutions and people setting targets for accountability may not easily be held accountable themselves if the targets can be varied with little or no effective scrutiny. And if the numbers used to deliver accountability on any given target are opaquely manipulable by actors with a stake in being able to claim success, it is hard to take such claims at face value.

'Leave No One Behind'

The 2013 report to the UN Secretary-General of the High Level Panel of Eminent Persons on the Post-2015

Development Agenda proved to be highly influential. It set out 'five transformative shifts', of which the first – and the only one still referred to in the terms of that report – is to 'Leave no one behind'. The report trod a difficult line, on the one hand emphasizing continuity from the MDGs, while, on the other, seeking greater ambition and highlighting the extent to which a concern with social exclusion represents a significant innovation:

> The next development agenda must ensure that in the future neither income nor gender, nor ethnicity, nor disability, nor geography, will determine whether people live or die, whether a mother can give birth safely, or whether her child has a fair chance in life. We must keep faith with the promise of the MDGs and now finish the job. The MDGs aspired to halve poverty. After 2015 we should aspire to put an end to hunger and extreme poverty as well as addressing poverty in all its other forms. This is a major new commitment to everyone on the planet who feels marginalized or excluded, and to the neediest and most vulnerable people, to make sure their concerns are addressed and that they can enjoy their human rights. ...
>
> To be sure that our actions are helping not just the largest number of people, but the neediest and most vulnerable, we will need *new ways of measuring success.*[22]

The main shift in development thought since the MDGs were put in place has been the continuing rise to prominence of inequalities as a key challenge. One contribution to that has been what is arguably the MDGs' biggest success, MDG 3: Promote gender equality and empower women.

This fixed in place what was in 2000 an emerging norm. Depending on your point of view, the single target – 'To eliminate gender disparity in primary and secondary education by 2005, and in all levels of education by 2015' – either was admirably focused in one area in which it was feasible to construct data, and thereby ensured demonstrable change; or was focused on such a partial interpretation of the goal as to actively restrict progress. In either case, the goal strengthened the demands for gender equality to be met in a much wider range of areas – and for the relevant data architecture to be put in place.

The gender equality goal also confirmed the technical and political potential to address other group inequalities in such development targets. Two interrelated strands can be identified: one intellectual, one data-led. Great credit must be given to the pioneering work of Frances Stewart on horizontal inequalities and of Naila Kabeer on intersecting inequalities.[23] Alongside this, the growing availability of relatively consistent household survey data has allowed a range of group inequalities to be analysed. Although the data remained (and remains) far from perfect, the effect was to demonstrate the possibility of a truly global framework with disaggregation in multiple dimensions – just as minds were beginning to turn towards thoughts of a successor to the MDGs.

In the writing of Christian Aid's 2010 report, *We're All in This Together*, a range of indicative data on group inequalities within MDG targets was used. It showed, for example, the excess mortality ratios facing children born into indigenous groups in a range of countries, and the extent to which education, household wealth and rural/urban location shape access to contraception or child malnutrition.[24] My brief spell working at Save the Children coincided with the global thematic consultations on the post-2015 framework.[25] As our efforts were focused on strengthening the approach to inequalities, we began to assemble a more comprehensive dataset from household surveys to show their strengths and limitations.

Figure 1 draws from the subsequently published *GRID* (Group-based Inequalities Database) and provides a simple example of the power of disaggregation. The three panels highlight multiple points, in the almost arbitrarily chosen context of the completion of lower secondary education by India's young people. First, the national level is around 70 per cent. Second, there is something of a gender split: a differential of around five percentage points between

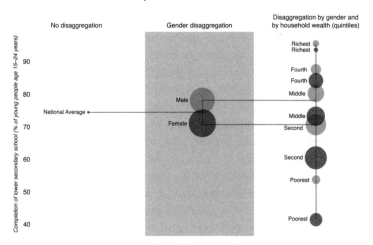

Figure 1: Counting is power: gender and wealth disaggregation of Indian lower secondary school completion

Source: Save the Children's Group-based Inequalities Database (GRID): https://campaigns.savethechildren.net/grid.

boys (higher completion) and girls. It is only when we consider the intersection of gender and household wealth (by quintile) that the most striking results, in the third panel, become visible. Girls are disproportionately located in the least wealthy three quintiles; and their (average) completion rates here are 65 per cent or below. Boys are disproportionately located in the wealthiest three quintiles, and their (average) completion rates range from nearly 70 per cent up to 90 per cent.

The prospects for policy improvement are strikingly better when the three panels are in view, as opposed to just the first or second. So too is the potential to hold policymakers to account for addressing inequalities. And now imagine that the same dataset would allow further disaggregation by region, by urban/rural location, by religion, by scheduled caste and tribe, and by the presence of disabilities. What inequalities, what policy-crucial information and priorities would be revealed? This was the dynamic that informed the debates on the post-2015 framework, and much of the optimism of those engaged in them.

At the same time, there was a fierce battle over the extent to which vertical inequality should be targeted. A pivotal moment in development debates had occurred since the MDGs were put in place, with data at the heart of it. Former World Bank economist Paul Collier's *The Bottom Billion: Why the Poorest Countries are Failing and What Can Be Done About It* came out in 2007 and set a new bar for the profile and influence of development writing. But the book can also be seen as the last great defence of an approach that was already outdated by then. Collier focused on countries with low average per capita incomes, and laid out a series of poverty 'traps' that could be overcome by careful intervention by policymakers.

The book's main thesis was subsequently demolished in Andy Sumner's (2010) work on the 'new bottom billion', which took advantage of relatively newly available distribution data to show that the majority of extreme income poverty actually occurred in middle- rather than low-income countries – and had done for some time. Sumner demonstrated that this was due primarily to within-country income inequality, rather than countries' absolute poverty. A quite different set of policy responses follows, once the problem is understood as an inequality 'trap' instead.[26]

The power of this analysis combined with growing political attention to income and wealth inequalities in donor countries following the 2008 financial crisis, and the economically unjustifiable 'austerity' policies that many governments imposed in response. There remained powerful resistance to hard targets on income (and wealth) inequality, both within and between countries, as explored in Chapter 5 below. But the process to set what would become the UN Sustainable Development Goals (SDGs), a framework set to run from 2016 to 2030, was much more open and participative than had been its predecessor – and inequality was a constant topic.

The process established something much closer to a global conversation (albeit with inevitable issues of access and empowered engagement) than the 'few white men in a room' approach that developed the MDG framework from the original Millennium Declaration. In keeping with this wider ownership, the financing emphasis is very much on domestic resource mobilization (and on tax revenues in particular), rather than on foreign aid – crucial to ensure that national priorities determine the local application of the global framework.

In the broader context of development thought, the SDGs represent an entirely logical evolution from the MDGs – and one largely signposted by the summary in Table 1 above. Where the MDGs combined the then-dominant monetary poverty and capabilities approaches, the SDGs add important social exclusion dynamics to the framework and in the process put somewhat greater emphasis on participatory approaches – or at least the principles of national ownership, and policy independence.

Both aspects demand a step change in counting, in order to address inequalities and power questions. They require data to capture important group disaggregations, as well as data to provide transparency and support accountability. If MDG 3 both reflected and confirmed the understanding that gender-blindness was not gender-neutral, it was increasingly widely understood that the failure to count was also likely to be regressive with respect to other group inequalities. And so the SDGs were presented under the banner of 'Leave No One Behind', and this was made concrete with the commitment that no target will be considered met until it is met for each relevant group within the given population.

Reflecting the recognition that development is global, rather than the province of countries below some arbitrary level of per capita income, the set of 17 goals, 169 targets and a still-emerging set of indicators to run until 2030 is universal (that is, it includes high-income countries).

Goal 1 End poverty in all its forms everywhere
Goal 2 End hunger, achieve food security and improved nutrition and promote sustainable agriculture

Goal 3   Ensure healthy lives and promote well-being for all at all ages

Goal 4   Ensure inclusive and equitable quality education and promote lifelong learning opportunities for all

Goal 5   Achieve gender equality and empower all women and girls

Goal 6   Ensure availability and sustainable management of water and sanitation for all

Goal 7   Ensure access to affordable, reliable, sustainable and modern energy for all

Goal 8   Promote sustained, inclusive and sustainable economic growth, full and productive employment and decent work for all

Goal 9   Build resilient infrastructure, promote inclusive and sustainable industrialization and foster innovation

Goal 10   Reduce inequality within and among countries

Goal 11   Make cities and human settlements inclusive, safe, resilient and sustainable

Goal 12   Ensure sustainable consumption and production patterns

Goal 13   Take urgent action to combat climate change and its impacts

Goal 14   Conserve and sustainably use the oceans, seas and marine resources for sustainable development

Goal 15   Protect, restore and promote sustainable use of terrestrial ecosystems, sustainably manage forests, combat desertification, and halt and reverse land degradation and halt biodiversity loss

Goal 16   Promote peaceful and inclusive societies for sustainable development, provide access to justice for all and build effective, accountable and inclusive institutions at all levels

Goal 17   Strengthen the means of implementation and revitalize the Global Partnership for Sustainable Development (including finance; technology; capacity-building; trade; and systemic issues)

The two aims of global goals identified by Fukuda-Parr for the MDGs remain: to set norms and incentives, and to communicate social objectives. The SDGs represent an enormously ambitious and important framework for global policy – and one that reflects the major shifts in development thinking, putting inequalities at the centre of the challenge.

But development's data problem also remains, for while the new framework is in part a response to the significant progress made in counting, it also creates unprecedented demands on the underlying data. The technical challenges to which these give rise have led to calls for a data revolution – but the political imperative for an overthrow of our statistical approaches is not as widely appreciated. Just as with GDP, there are grave risks that targeting development on the basis of indicators assumed to be unbiased will introduce major distortions to policy and progress – because of who and what go uncounted.

2

The 'Data Revolution'

Data: *Facts and statistics collected together for reference or analysis*
Revolution: *A forcible overthrow of a government or social order, in favour of a new system*
Oxford English Dictionary

This chapter lays out the threat of the uncounted to development, and the need for urgent technical and political response.

The term 'uncounted' is used to describe a politically motivated failure to count. This takes two main forms. First, there may be people and groups at the bottom of distributions (e.g., income) whose 'uncounting' adds another level to their marginalization – for example, where they are absent from statistics that inform policy prioritization. Second, there may be people and groups at the top of distributions who are further empowered by being able to go uncounted – not least by hiding income and wealth from taxation and regulation.

In either case, the phenomenon is not a random or arbitrary one. Being uncounted is not generally a matter of coincidence, but reflects power: the lack of it, or its excess.

As such, the term 'data revolution' is highly appropriate. The implication is not of a technical reform, but rather of a radical political change. If the UN SDGs were to reach their potential in this regard, they would drive a major redistribution of power – and with it, a major reduction in poverty. But a purely technocratic approach will fail – because, as Frederick Douglass knew, power does not willingly concede.[1]

The central framework for global efforts to improve people's lives is the 2030 Agenda for Sustainable Development.[2] Underpinning this are the SDGs, a key element of which is the 'data revolution'. In 2013, the UN global thematic consultation on inequalities concluded that success would require

> measures to strengthen the capacity and coverage of national and sub-national monitoring and evaluation, data collection and analysis. These will need to track the impact of policies, legislation, budgets and programmes among those most disadvantaged and excluded; allow for truly participatory assessment of these measures; enable much more systematic disaggregation of information for equity-focused targets and indicators; and provide mechanisms for locally-led citizen monitoring and feedback on progress and performance.[3]

Later that year, the High Level Panel of Eminent Persons confirmed to the UN Secretary-General that 'any new goals should be accompanied by an independent and rigorous monitoring system, [requiring] a *data revolution* for sustainable development, with a new international initiative to improve the quality of statistics and information available to people and governments'.[4]

A major criticism of the MDGs reflected here is that, by largely ignoring identity, and targeting aggregate progress instead, the framework actually incentivized greater inequality. In the simplest case of vertical inequalities in extreme monetary poverty, helping those living on US$0.01 a day reach a dollar a day is almost inevitably harder than tipping those on US$0.99 a day over the line instead.

The evidence shows that countries that reduced horizontal inequalities tended to see greater aggregate success (e.g., in child mortality reduction[5]), but this was not obvious *ex ante*. Where existing inequalities reflected the balance of power in a country, and/or were not widely recognized, then a well-meaning pursuit of national progress could easily exacerbate or simply fail to address them. UNICEF published a forthright analysis in 2015 calling for the lessons of the MDGs to be learnt, and to stop the 'vicious cycles of intergenerational disadvantage' that result from a failure to do 'a better job in collecting and using data to find out who the most vulnerable and excluded children are and where they can be found'.[6]

Even the MDGs' one group inequality success story, the gender norm-setting of MDG 3, did not seem to have led to broad progress in counting. As of 2013, a report for the UN Secretary-General found that just one in eight countries had a dedicated gender statistics budget.[7]

The failures are political as well as technical, as the case of Sudan discussed below demonstrates dramatically. The technical level is important, however, and the social exclusion impetus of the SDGs is intended to ensure that identity is well recognized from the outset; and that disaggregated data support accountability for addressing group inequalities.

The last of the 169 targets in the SDGs, from goal 17, which addresses the means of implementation, are as follows:

Data, monitoring and accountability
17.18 By 2020, enhance capacity-building support to developing countries, including for least developed countries and small island developing States, to increase significantly the availability of high-quality, timely and reliable data disaggregated by income, gender, age, race, ethnicity, migratory status, disability, geographic location and other characteristics relevant in national contexts

17.19   By 2030, build on existing initiatives to develop measurements of progress on sustainable development that complement gross domestic product, and support statistical capacity-building in developing countries

At first glance, these are fantastic – light years ahead of the MDGs. But looking a little closer quickly gives reasons for caution. Why we should wait until 2030 to sort out GDP is not clear, although that is a big ship to turn, so perhaps this is not unreasonable. But the real lacuna is about accountability. Like the MDGs, and goal 8 in particular on global partnership, it is not clear who will actually deliver any of this – but at the same time, each point is written from a donor perspective rather than one of all countries as equal participants.

Two main risks can be identified: first, that the core data necessary simply is not collected; and second, that the data is collected but is characterized by such systematic weaknesses as to undermine the aims of inclusion from the outset.

Technical Challenges

Analysis to date has largely focused on the first risk, and on the technical and financial aspects (rather than the political ones). Probably the most common interpretation of the 'data revolution' call has been as requiring a major increase in the coverage and frequency of household surveys – in order to establish that *'neither income nor gender, nor ethnicity, nor disability, nor geography'* remains a determinant of major human development outcomes.[8]

Much of the public discussion at this point focused on the financial feasibility of such an approach. Morten Jerven suggested in 2014 that the costs of such a survey push would be prohibitive. Estimating the cost of a full MDG data package at around US$1 billion a year, he extrapolated on a simple per-target basis to suggest a total figure for the SDGs of as much as US$254 billion (or around two and a half times the global, annual aid budget). Analysis from the Center for Global Development concluded that this was greatly overblown. In practice, it was suggested that the total of international donor assistance needed would be of the order of US$300 million per year – much of it already provided, so not an additional cost for the SDGs.[9]

Much less prominently analysed in the post-2015 context has been the range of systematic weaknesses in current survey and national census data. Here, the work of Roy Carr-Hill has been ground-breaking in assessing the extent to which six particular groups are excluded, either by design or by sampling failures.[10]

Three groups are excluded by design from household surveys, by dint of not being part of households: homeless populations; those in institutions (hospitals and prisons); and highly mobile populations, including nomadic and pastoralist groups. A further three groups are underrepresented to an important degree through sampling failures: those living in informal settlements; those from households that are fragile and/or disjointed; and those living in relatively insecure areas.

Overall, albeit using inevitably somewhat crude estimates, Carr-Hill identifies the potential scale of the problem as affecting some 300–350 million people.[11] World population was then estimated to stand at around 7 billion people, so the scale of exclusions would approach the 5 per cent level that accountants typically use to indicate a material issue in company financial reports. If this was a material but randomly distributed under-sampling, it might not be such a grave concern, but a common feature of the groups in question is the likelihood of their being overwhelmingly overrepresented at the bottom of the relevant income distributions.

To put that another way: in the household surveys that are widely seen as the best hope that the SDG data revolution leaves no one behind, the uncounted are not random, but are systematically from marginalized and vulnerable populations: the left behind.

A striking illustration of the implications for a single development indicator is provided by Carr-Hill's estimates for the access to water of urban populations in sub-Saharan Africa. Allowing for the estimated 40 million people uncounted in informal settlements, Carr-Hill models a scenario in which the uncounted are all in the lowest income group and none has access to improved water sources. Compared to UN figures in which 54 million people (17 per cent of 324 million people) have no improved water source, this implies the true figure may be as high as 95 million (26 per cent of the new total of 364 million people).

A quite separate failing of survey data relates to the identities that are – or are not – captured. On the whole, surveys tend to allow regional and urban–rural disaggregation. Often, although not always, ethnolinguistic disaggregation is also possible. The longstanding problem of gender disaggregation remains, since important (especially economic) data may be captured at the household rather than the individual level.

Perhaps the most egregious failing of surveys in respect of the groups identified in the SDGs – or indeed elsewhere – relates to people living with disabilities. The failures are consistent with those related to mental health and old age, and if anything appear to be worsening over time.

Emma Samman and Laura Rodriguez-Takeuchi summarized the evidence in 2013.[12] People over the age of 60 make up 11 per cent of the global population (and perhaps double that by 2050), and the households they head are likely to have lower incomes. An estimated 15–20 per cent of the world's population lives with some form of disability, including those resulting from mental health issues, and the disability is considered severe for an estimated 2–4 per cent of the global population. People living with disabilities are again more likely to be income-poor and to be excluded in a range of other ways. A more recent study published in *The Lancet* suggests the underlying numbers may be much worse, and that, due to apathy, they are effectively uncounted. This especially pernicious set of failures is addressed in more detail in the following chapter.

Samman and Rodriguez-Takeuchi also show that the three groups (i.e., old age, disability, mental health) are undercounted, and often completely uncounted, in the main surveys conducted. There are issues in terms of coverage (for example, these groups may be more likely to live outside formal households, a problem discussed above) and the extent of information collected (not least, whose opinion is sought about conditions affecting household members).

The biggest issues, however, relate to identification. Are the right questions being asked in surveys, of sufficient numbers of people to obtain representative data? Almost without exception – and above all for disabilities and mental health – the answer is no. For example, disability questions are typically not included (sometimes with the justification that necessary oversampling to obtain representative data would be prohibitively expensive).

Where disability questions have been included, the form has been weak. For example: 'Is [NAME] physically or mentally handicapped or disabled?' Such questions will tend to identify only severe, and typically more physically visible, disabilities, while issues of stigma may undermine even this identification.

There is now fairly broad consensus – although only limited practical use – of the minimum six-question approach proposed by the UN's Washington Group on Statistics, which instead puts the emphasis on self-reporting of actual capabilities:

Because of a physical, mental, or emotional health condition ...
1. Do you have difficulty seeing even if wearing glasses?
2. Do you have difficulty hearing even if using hearing aid/s or are you deaf?
3. Do you have difficulty walking or climbing stairs?
4. Do you have difficulty remembering or concentrating?

5. Do you have difficulty (with self-care such as) washing all over or dressing?
6. Do you have difficulty communicating (for example, understanding or being understood by others)?
Question response categories: No, Some, A lot, and Unable.]

Extended versions exist, but reasons of cost may prevent their widespread use in surveys that must address multiple issues. As of the Washington Group's annual meeting in November 2018, 95 countries had used these or similar questions in some way (including in 'census, national survey, disability module, or pre-test') and 32 countries plan to use the questions in their next census.[13]

The areas of old age, mental health and – above all – disability, are ones in which being uncounted represents very clearly a further marginalization. Progress will require new approaches that condemn such exclusion to the past. Without the data to assess whether these groups are included in any individual SDG achievements, there is little or no chance that they will be.

Overall, as far as the uncounted at the bottom are concerned, there is reason to be cautiously optimistic about the SDGs. The driving force of the social exclusion approach has resulted in a clear focus on group inequalities, and so the proposed data revolution may go a long way to improving identity-based development statistics.

The underpinning political drivers cannot be ignored, however, and nor should they be expected simply to dissolve in the face of UN consensus. There is no coincidence in the fact that so many of the groups about whom data is now sought, but currently unavailable, have been unable to exert the effective political demand to be counted.

This may reflect a widespread lack of understanding or concern from others, for example, as is likely to be the case worldwide for persons living with disabilities. It may reflect embedded political dynamics, for example such as that facing indigenous peoples. The statistics here provide a sad confirmation of marginalization. From the late 1980s, the estimates cited are of a total population of around 300 million, in more than 70 countries across all the regions of the world. For more than a decade, including an unreferenced World Bank paper from 1999 that has subsequently been cited repeatedly, these figures continue to be used. As far as I have been able to uncover, the first use of the statistics is associated with the International Labour Organization (ILO), around the promotion of its Convention concerning Indigenous and Tribal Peoples in Independent Countries of 1989, and which came into force in 1991. The UN Economic and Social Council (ECOSOC) Working Group on Indigenous Populations also referenced similar numbers during this period.[14]

The UN 'backgrounder' for the 'historic first session of the new Permanent Forum on Indigenous Issues' in May 2002 also uses the same estimates, at least 13 years after they were first published, and itself becomes a commonly cited reference in subsequent years.[15] By 2007, with the UN Declaration on the Rights of Indigenous Peoples, the estimates had risen to 370 million people in around 90 countries, and these figures continue to be widely used.

This 5–6 per cent of the world's population is estimated to account for around 15 per cent of the global population living in extreme income poverty. But even this most basic quantification is not straightforward; in part because of the continuing failure of states to value indigenous populations, and in part because of genuine complexities. According to the UN Permanent Forum on Indigenous Issues:[16]

> Considering the diversity of indigenous peoples, an official definition of 'indigenous' has not been adopted by any UN-system body. Instead the system has developed a modern understanding of this term based on the following:
> - Self-identification as indigenous peoples at the individual level and accepted by the community as their member.
> - Historical continuity with pre-colonial and/or pre-settler societies.

- Strong link to territories and surrounding natural resources.
- Distinct social, economic or political systems.
- Distinct language, culture and beliefs.
- Form non-dominant groups of society.
- Resolve to maintain and reproduce their ancestral environments and systems as distinctive peoples and communities.

Greater attention is slowly being given to what the UN Special Rapporteur refers to as 'nearly universal disadvantageous social and economic conditions' facing indigenous peoples.[17] But there is a disturbing consistency in the major UN assessments. The UN General Assembly commemorated the launch of the International Year of the World's Indigenous People in 1992, highlighting the 'continuing need to improve the availability and the means of dissemination of socioeconomic data relating to the development needs of indigenous people'.[18] Twenty-five years later, the 2017 Ministerial Declaration of the UN High Level Political Forum was (rightly) commended by the International Work Group for Indigenous Affairs for having 'repeated the need for data disaggregation by ethnicity, which is critical for indigenous peoples to be visible in monitoring the achievements and gaps in the implementation of the SDGs'.[19]

We can – and should – celebrate commitments from the likes of the UK's Department for International Development (DFID) to the Inclusive Data Charter Principles. But at the same time, we need to be clear that the reasons not to count are ultimately political. If the politics haven't changed, then technical processes will not deliver – at least not without touching the question of who owns data and collection processes.

Principle 1: All populations must be included in the data.
Principle 2: All data should, wherever possible, be disaggregated in order to accurately describe all populations.

Principle 3: Data should be drawn from all available sources.

Principle 4: Those responsible for the collection of data and production of statistics must be accountable.

Principle 5: Human and technical capacity to collect, analyse and use disaggregated data needs to be improved, including through adequate and sustainable financing.

There is a legitimate analogy with medical research here. The Declaration of Helsinki is intended to govern this, and sets out that a trial involving a disadvantaged or vulnerable population or community is only justified if the research is responsive to the health needs and priorities of this population or community and if there is a reasonable likelihood that this population or community stands to benefit from the results of the research.[20] Is it time for a similarly explicit ethical charter in relation to the collection of human development data?

Look again at the final targets of the SDGs. The commitments to data disaggregation are the basis for the targets that make 'Leave no one behind' more than a slogan. But the framing reflects a clear power differential already: *we*, the donors, will help them, the recipients, to sort out *their* bad data. This would stick in the craw a little less if 'high-quality, timely and reliable data disaggregated by income, gender, age, race, ethnicity, migratory status, disability, geographic location and other characteristics relevant in national contexts' was consistently available in high-income countries. But this is far from the case, and the risk is that target 17.18 becomes another one where 'we' tried to help, but 'they' couldn't manage – rather than a truly shared enterprise with full and equal national accountabilities, as the SDGs are supposed to be.

This chapter has so far spent time on the more technical aspects – reasons why the MDGs did not address inequalities, and why the SDGs may perhaps struggle. But the clearest reasons are the blatantly political ones: that governments all too often do not care to address inequalities, or indeed actively promote them; and that, despite what it says on the label, international development efforts are not (solely) driven by aims of human progress.

Power Concedes Nothing

Yes, it's fucking political. Everything's political.
                                               Skunk Anansie[21]

When I was a young boy, I remember an occasional visitor to our house: a very tall, thin man with the longest fingers I'd ever seen. I had cause to remember him better in later years, because when he took a job elsewhere he gave my brother and me the set of encyclopaedias that he had been building up. (Note for younger readers: encyclopaedias were an alternative source of knowledge before wikis or indeed the internet existed.)

Fast forward a couple of decades, and in the early 2000s I found myself working as a researcher at Queen Elizabeth House, the University of Oxford's Department of International Development. By happy chance, I learned that in late 2004 I would coincide on a trip abroad with this man I hadn't seen for 20 years. And so I searched him online (who needs encyclopaedias these days? And yet ...).

Abdullahi El-Tom is a Sudanese sociologist at the National University of Ireland in Maynooth, who has written extensively about the Berti people of northern Darfur, one of the poorest regions of Sudan. Since February 2003 at least, the government had been conducting a campaign of genocidal ethnic cleansing in the region of Darfur (and elsewhere), using both its own military forces and a militia proxy, the Janjaweed. Estimates of fatalities by late 2004 had climbed to 70,000 people, with estimates that more than 2 million had been displaced.

El-Tom had recently written about the 'Black Book' of Sudan, or, to give it its full title, 'The Black Book: Imbalance of Power and Wealth in Sudan'. Written anonymously and circulated in secret from 2000, the Black Book made the case that the country had been governed since British colonial rule in a way marked by profound regional inequalities. It quickly came to be a central text for those opposed to the government in Khartoum, providing a platform for common alliances (rather than, for example, religious, racial or cultural differences), and the subsequent formal alliance between the Justice and Equality Movement (JEM), to which El-Tom had been an adviser, and which was said to include at least some of the Black Book's authors, and the Sudan Liberation Movement/Army.

While foreign media coverage was dominated by views of the conflict as racial ('Arab' against 'African') and religious (the Muslim north against the largely Christian and animist south), rebel groups united around the Black Book's claims of regional discrimination:

> Sudan was not ideal at its Independence in 1956. Resources were poorly divided among different provinces at the time. By the 1970s some progress was made and gaps between provinces started narrowing. The last two decades have been different. Resources were moved to concentrate in the Northern and Central Regions leading to impoverishment of other Regions. ... Destruction of marginalized Regions has become a feature of Sudan, particularly during the reign of [the] current Regime.[22]

El-Tom argued that Northern Sudanese took their opportunity at independence in claiming a fitness to lead that stemmed from their scientific rationality, as opposed to the barbarism of other Sudanese. This was justified by a political discourse of 'Arabization', which over time became closely linked to Islam, and provided the justification for the elite's claims to dominance, just as Edward Said set out in his seminal book, *Orientalism*. The colonial project rested on the imposition of social relations that contrasted the modern, rational, scientific, disciplined (empire) with the backward, uncontrolled (subject). With the end of the Anglo-Egyptian rule of 1898–1956, the economically privileged Northern Sudanese adopted the position of colonialists.

El-Tom writes:

[I]t was not the simple claim to Arab ancestry which elevated [Northern] Sudan to its hegemonic position in the country. Rather, it was their opportunistic monopolisation of modernity that was once the preserve of British colonial staff. By appropriating modernity and becoming its overseers in the Sudan, they have succeeded in dislodging many other ethnic groups across the Sudan who can mobilise their claim to Arab ancestry. Nomadic groups like the Kababish, the Ziyadiya, the Rashaida and the Zibaidiya can all profess Arab identity to an extent that cannot be matched by the current hegemonic groups in the country. However, in the current discourse of power, they are classified as essentially backwards and at odds with modernity.[23]

The authors of the Black Book sought to show the effect of this discourse on access to power in the Sudan. To do this, they determined the regional (rather than, say, ethnolinguistic) origins of each minister appointed in each government from independence in 1956 until 2000, and compared it with the underlying population distribution. The data they gathered (leading to suspicions that the authors may have held posts in Khartoum themselves) shows how the ministerial share of the Northern region varied between 60 per cent and 80 per cent, with the sole exception of the second democratic period (1986–9) when the share fell to 47 per cent. The Northern region's population makes up *less than 5 per cent* of Sudan's total.

A second volume of the Black Book, published in 2002, went on to claim that this disproportionate access to power had real impacts on Sudan, through concomitantly disproportionate provision of government support, which unfairly reduced the human development opportunities of the marginalized regions. This was the claim I decided to test, and so set about compiling data on Sudanese government finances and development at the regional level.[24] Between official data, IMF, World Bank and various UN sources, including the UN Population Fund, it was possible to trace the regional patterns from the 1990s of revenue-raising, expenditure and of some basic human development indicators.

The patterns were clear. On the fiscal side, only the capital, Khartoum, exceeded the Northern region in government expenditure per capita. Other regions saw per capita expenditures of between 40 per cent (Darfur in the west) and 70 per cent (the east) of the level of the north. Expenditures marked for development showed an even more extreme bias, with the west receiving just 17 per cent of the level of the north.

Outcomes were closely tied. Infant mortality in all other regions was between 20 per cent and 50 per cent higher than in the north and Khartoum, while the percentage of births attended by specialists was much lower. Primary school enrolment and literacy rates were as low elsewhere as half of the levels seen in the north. The data allowed me also to track changes in literacy from 1993 to 2002, and so to assess the changes under the 1989 dictatorship. While literacy rates in the north rose by 10 per cent, they fell everywhere else: in the Central region (even including Khartoum) by 2.6 per cent, in the east by 13.8 per cent and in the west by 10.2 per cent. Male literacy fell by a third in the west, compared to just 3 per cent in the north.

I wrote:

> There can be no doubt that the current dictatorship has been pernicious for the human development of the regions outside of the North and Khartoum. There can be no question that the data support the claims made in the Black Book that the Sudan has been governed to benefit those

regions disproportionately at the expense of all others – who account for 80% of the population, or around 25 million people.[25]

And there this story might rest. These research findings were cited in a range of other work – including the Wikipedia entry on the Black Book, which has a certain historical rhyme with Abdullahi's gift. But nothing changed: there was no greater accountability for the government of Sudan despite the Black Book setting the context for much of the country-wide opposition. Some 15 years later, Bashir has finally been forced to stand down but, at the time of writing, the military regime is still clinging to power.[26]

We might file this under 'research paper fails to change world', shrug and move on. But there is a footnote to the story that makes the point about the uncounted rather more clearly. When the IMF published a report nearly ten years later using a wide range of new regional data, I requested access to it.[27] The IMF staff delayed repeatedly, including passing me to more senior colleagues. I was given to believe that the Sudanese government was doing the same in response to the IMF's request for permission: permission, that is, to publish data that they already had as part of their monitoring duties. Ultimately, the data was not made available to me – or, presumably, to any Sudanese citizen with an interest in exploring the regional discrimination of their own government. Is it legitimate for an international institution, far less one with a development aim, to receive such basic data from a state, but to hold it privately?

Subsequently, both the World Bank and UNDP have managed to obtain and publish further data. The World Bank study of 2014 lays out the exact divergence between the government's approach and an allocation formula based on population or poverty.[28] North Darfur, for example, would see a 91 per cent increase in its allocation under a poverty-based allocation formula; South Darfur would see a 236 per cent increase. An independent 2017 study of fiscal decentralisation in Sudan carried out for the Chr. Michelsen Institute in Norway concludes as follows:

> A small group of ruling elite control Sudan's governance structures. The ruling elite command strategic resources and preside over the state in ways that produce conflict with major societal groups. Combined economic and political failures threaten the state with dismemberment and disintegration. Furthermore, the decay and failure of state institutions and a polarised political environment threaten further territorial disintegration.
>
> High vertical fiscal imbalances (that is, gaps between spending and revenues at the state level) and horizontal fiscal imbalances (that is, imbalances across the states) make the allocation of transfers to states appear biased and unfair.[29]

Where governments are set on deepening particular inequalities, or not addressing them, it is optimistic to the point of foolishness to think that those same governments will facilitate willingly the data to lay bare their intention. And when transparency becomes an act of sedition, international and intergovernmental organizations may not be reliably on the side of counting.

If there is to be a revolution in development statistics – a 'forcible overthrow' of the existing system – it will not come in the form of technical solutions alone, however rigorous or well-meaning. The data 'revolution' that is needed must be a revolution indeed: not (just) a gradual process of dealing with technical difficulties, but a radical and deeply political challenge to the power structures that lie behind the uncounted.

The data from where the SDGs begin are, indeed, revolting. Consider just some of the marginalized groups discussed above: indigenous peoples, people living with disabilities, and the six groups excluded from household surveys. Their quantification – even a simple tally – is imperfect, a confirmation of these groups' uncountedness. In total, however, they are estimated to account for 25–30 per cent of the world population – and a much higher share of people living in extreme income poverty.

Consider, next, that the inequalities faced are not mutually exclusive. Allowing for overlap among the groups will reduce the total number of people – but those facing intersectional inequalities are likely to face, on average, even deeper poverty. And consider, finally, that there is a whole set of layered inequalities on top of these: other intersecting inequalities including importantly gender, and also other dimensions, including political exclusion.

3
We the People – But Only Some of Them

The federal government has to know that we exist – what we do, what we have ... Before, we were totally forgotten. Now equality is coming through the census.

Jorge Moreira de Oliveira, of the Kalunga quilombo, Brazil, in 2010[1]

In reckoning the numbers of the people of the Commonwealth, or of a State or other part of the Commonwealth, aboriginal natives shall not be counted.

Commonwealth of Australia Constitution Act (1900)

We the People of the United States, in Order to form a more perfect Union, establish Justice, insure domestic Tranquility, provide for the common defence, promote the general Welfare, and secure the Blessings of Liberty to ourselves and our Posterity, do ordain and establish this Constitution for the United States of America.

...

Representatives and direct Taxes shall be apportioned among the several States which may be included within this Union, according to their respective Numbers, which shall be determined by adding to the whole Number of free Persons, including those bound to Service for a Term of

Years, and excluding Indians not taxed, three fifths of all other Persons.

Constitution of the United States of America
(1787).

This chapter makes the case that the data most important to political outcomes, including census data, birth registration and voter rolls, is especially vulnerable to uncounting – including in the world's biggest and richest economies.

The history of colonized countries in particular is replete with examples of the deliberate uncounting of occupied populations, and of less valued groups. It also provides the most dramatic examples of the dynamic interplay for marginalized groups between two competing impulses. On the one hand, groups may seek to be counted in order to be (somewhat) empowered to make demands on the state. On the other hand, groups may actively resist being counted in order to avoid the illegitimate state's demands on them.

The constitutional texts cited above, from Australia and the United States of America, represent the outcomes of political processes designed to overcome conflict. In the US case, the 13 states then negotiating over the terms of their union had to reach agreement over, among other things, their relative tax contributions to the centre and their relative political representation there. Apportioning taxing responsibilities and political power jointly on the basis of population was the solution chosen, with the aim of mitigating any incentives to game the system. If a state sought to undercount its population with the aim of artificially lowering its tax contribution, it would also lose political representation – while a state seeking to inflate its representation by overcounting population would have to pay for doing so.[2]

The relationship between census-taking and tax-raising is long established, perhaps most famously as a tool of the Roman Empire. Then and since, the twin desires of a 'modern' state both to quantify society and to extract revenue from it (and/or conscripts to fight wars), have often triggered public scepticism. The evidence shows that greater state reliance on tax revenues is associated, over time, with improvements in political representation – while reliance on natural resource wealth, in contrast, often leads to greater corruption and less inclusive representation.[3] But this relationship rests on the greater accountability that citizens demand, when their financial contribution to the state is more salient (or painful) – so, for example, the relationship has sometimes been shown to be stronger for direct taxes such as those on income, than the less obvious indirect taxes (e.g., those on trade or consumption).[4]

When a state of questionable legitimacy introduces census measures, and when these are understood to be tied to taxation, the political response may simply be rejection. The year 1852 saw two cases of this, on opposite sides of the Atlantic.

In Gold Coast (now Ghana), the British imperial administration led an assembly of elders and chiefs to agree a poll tax of one shilling for each man, woman and child. The situation was complicated by the British government's reluctance to take formal responsibility for the Gold Coast, for various reasons, hence its remaining a protectorate. The Secretary of State for the Colonies, the third Earl Grey, had sought a way for the region to raise its own funds. Recognizing the risk of resistance, Grey had argued that a direct tax could be accepted if it 'were light, if it were spent in the districts where it was raised, if the people could see tangible results in the shape of roads, schools and hospitals, [and] if the chiefs were closely associated with the raising and spending of the money'.[5]

In practice, with Grey having moved on, the process worked quite differently. The historian G. E. Metcalfe summed up the result:

> [I]t was a travesty of [Grey's] plan that was put into operation. The tax itself was too onerous. The chiefs were not allowed to collect it for fear that they might oppress

their subjects. But the [British] government had no reliable agents of its own to do the job. There was still extortion, and it was hopeless for the government with its puny resources to try to collect the tax regularly independently of the chiefs. Nor were these consulted about spending the tax. Over a third of the proceeds were taken by the cost of collecting it. Most of what was left went in salaries. There was no doubt a case for increasing the pay of magistrates, but this benefit was least obvious to the people who paid ... As for the idea of a national representative assembly, that was completely lost sight of.[6]

Riots occurred in 1854 and again in 1857, and the tax – its revenue having fallen precipitously – was eliminated in 1864. Meanwhile, on the other side of the Atlantic – and on the other side of the global slave trade – a different type of counting had provoked similar unrest.

In what the sociologist Mara Loveman identifies as 'the only known instance of a popular uprising in direct response to the introduction of civil registration', Brazil saw mass uprisings until Decree 798 – making civil registration of births and deaths obligatory – was suspended at the end of January 1852.[7] Where Earl Grey may have recognized the absence of any legitimate state authority in Gold Coast, Loveman writes:

[The Brazilian state] was blinded by an illusion of state legitimacy and power that far surpassed actual state capacity. Brazil's political elite mistook the trappings of modernity in the imperial capital for the modern, territorial nation-state which they imagined – a state which had not yet been fully created, let alone consolidated. They mistook their own taken-for-granted commitment to 'progress' for popular willingness to embrace change. And once the uprising began, they mistook violent opposition to Decree 798 for evidence of the backwardness, irrationality, ignorance and stupidity of the poor, rural population.[8]

This Orientalist reading chimes with El-Tom's characterization of the Sudanese state since independence, and above all the 1989 regime. But it also points to a tension between the inclusive aims of the 'modern' state, and the potential for the rhetoric of modernity to exclude many.

The US and Australian constitutional documents cited above also show the explicit decision to give low or no weight to indigenous populations in the process of political apportionment between states within each country. To the extent that counting is performed to support government in decisions over 'who decides' and 'who gets what', exclusion is literal disempowerment.

While census representation – both as individuals and with a group identity – has been an aim for many, its value depends on the state in question being broadly legitimate. Being counted can represent a threat if the state is actively opposed to inclusion – from the efforts of the Nazi government in Germany to eradicate Jews and Roma, for example, to the South African apartheid regime's racial discrimination.

A policy stance of neutrality or 'blindness' towards significant group differences can play an important role in generating or maintaining exclusion – and if the data to show it are withheld, or not collated at all, then policy accountability will also be diminished. The attempts of the Bashir regime in Sudan to hide its ringfencing of development opportunities for a small part of the population has parallels, for example, with the refusal to track data on small groups known to be marginalized.

The inclusion in the 2000 census of many of Brazil's quilombolas (descendants of escaped African slaves, dating back in some cases to the sixteenth century) was followed by the Lula government's 2003 introduction of a quilombola programme aimed at ensuring the provision of basic public services, and a formal decree requiring identification and titling of land belonging to quilombo communities. Importantly, the identity of the quilombolas themselves was to be 'attested by self-definition'.[9] The next important step, already announced, is that the census of 2020 will directly capture the group identification of individuals.

This would allow unified statistics on the quilombolas to be created, as advocates have sought, rather than relying on the current estimates (e.g., of roughly 3,000 or 5,000 communities with 16 million members, and a poverty rate of around 75 per cent – three times as high as the national average).[10]

If there has been some progress on the census and public expenditure, land titling for quilombolas remains slow and contested. The land titles are crucial to ensure access to certain public services, including social housing, but also to resist private sector interests that vary from the construction sector in major urban areas, to mining and logging companies in the Amazon.

A 15-year legal battle against Lula's decree ended with a 2018 victory in the Supreme Court, which by a majority voted to uphold the right to self-identification for communities to qualify. But even so, serious obstacles remain. One rights group, Terra de Direitos, has estimated that, at the current rate of progress, the titling process would take 970 years to complete; while another, Justica Global, showed that the titling body has suffered a 93 per cent budget cut since 2013.[11] On top of this, at the start of his ultimately successful run for the presidency, Jair Bolsonaro promised that, if elected, he would put an end to all the indigenous reserves and quilombo communities, arguing that they should not be able to claim the natural resource wealth of the land.[12]

Brazil also provides important evidence of a complex issue around racial identification and the role of positive discrimination to address historic injustice. It seems clear that self-identification is central to better data – data that is more accurate, but also more legitimate and 'owned' in some important way by those being counted. But the process of identification is hardly neutral.

Following the 1852 uprising, it took Brazil 20 years before a full census was carried out, and it wasn't until the end of the century that civil registration was made obligatory. Another shift, away from inclusivity, was occurring at the same time. In the 1870s, Brazil's Diretoria Geral de Estatística (DGE) had focused on educational statistics as the key measure of national progress, supporting public spending on primary schools. But by the 1920s, as Loveman documents, a focus on Brazil's 'whiteness' had emerged as a standard of progress – despite the absence of questions on race from the census after 1872.

The 1888 abolition of slavery had, in one view, given rise to a greater concern with racial purity. The 1920 census report led with an essay that celebrated the 'Aryan immigration' from Europe, and the 'destruction of the black population in the extreme south'.[13] Some attributed the absence of race identification from the census as evidence of a desire to suppress knowledge of the country's racial mix, but the head of the DGE is quoted in that essay as saying that enumerators could not reliably distinguish between 'pure' whites and a 'whitish mulatto'; while self-identification is too subjective and would also introduce a bias towards whiteness. On that basis, including the question would inevitably weaken the scientific value of the results, and so it was excluded.

Racist states aside, the deeper question thrown up here is of the meaningfulness of identity characteristics including but not limited to race. At a practical level, the Washington Group questions on disability are designed to focus on simple factual responses – 'Do you have difficulty with X?', say, rather on the lines of 'Are you disabled?' – because the latter introduces a bias towards non-identification. In terms of race, or colour (because these have often been elided), identification questions are potentially more problematic, since the factual questions may not be obvious. What heritage, for example, would justify a given label? What, if any, labels are reasonable?

Census labels and other group-relevant policies of governments will contribute to the construction of identity categories, not only their counting. This means not only, as was found in South Africa, that the census 'has tended to reinforce the groups it was initially meant only to observe'. In Brazil, research on the interaction between the census and race-targeted affirmative action since the 2000s suggests that 'the Brazilian state is making race but not from scratch nor in ways that are fully intended' – in particular, that government categories are influencing self-identification patterns.[14]

Political scientist Rachel Gisselquist summarizes the findings of a special issue of the *Journal of Development Studies* on legal empowerment and group inequalities, including on the question of the 'fixity' of identities:

> [T]o the extent that we might be concerned about the real-world implications of such analysis – does it incentivise fixity in ethnic identification or mobilisation along ethnic lines? – it is worth highlighting two points. First, arguing for the relevance of an ethnic group-focused analysis of impact is not the same as arguing that legal empowerment policies should be designed to explicitly target ethnic groups in the manner, for instance, of affirmative action policies for ethnic minorities. Legal empowerment as understood here could be framed in more universalist terms while still having equalising impact among groups. Second, if we accept the constructivist proposition that ethnic boundaries may be constructed around economic and political differences, policies that lessen these differences should support, over time, a lessening of ethnic salience.[15]

Both affirmative action and broader strategies to redress historic inequalities, and (related or unrelated) reductions in the stigma associated with certain groups, are likely to lead to increasing self-identification, closing the uncounted gap. In the case of Australia, there has long been a significant gap with respect to indigenous peoples. The authors of a study from the Centre for Aboriginal Economic Policy Research note that these probably reflect the underlying sense of the state's legitimacy and propensity to act inclusively: 'People of Indigenous origin may choose not to disclose their ancestry for many reasons. Given Australia's history of discrimination against Indigenous people, including the removal of Indigenous children, fear of discrimination from the state is likely to be prominent among them.'[16]

Their analysis of Australian census returns for 2011 and 2016 show an increase in indigenous self-identification exceeding 80,000 people, or 13.7 per cent of the in-scope indigenous population at 2011 – meaning that 'the Indigenous population has always been much bigger than we previously thought. This is important not only for current policy, but also future planning, as we have no reason to expect that the process of identification change will not continue into the future.'[17]

South Africa provides a powerful case study of a discriminatory state's counting practices. Sociologists Akil Khalfani and Tukufu Zuberi survey the treatment of race from the first census of 1911, a year after the British creation of the Union of South Africa from its Cape of Good Hope, Orange Free State, Natal and Transvaal colonies, to the first post-apartheid census of 1996.[18] For racial identification, the underlying scheme of the state reflected both skin colour and ancestry. Table 3 reproduces Khalfani and Zuberi's summary of racial categories over time, and their source notes.

While self-classification was nominally in place, including where this involved selection of the appropriate form, notes for the 1936 survey show that the state had the final say: 'These [erroneous] entries are accepted to avoid giving offence and afterwards transferred to the correct form either by the Enumerator, the Supervisor or in the Census Office before tabulation.'[19] And in the South African state, racial classification was crucial not for eventual accountability around access to public services, but for the immediate possibilities that the law opened and closed as a result. In particular, the Population Registration Act assigned each person with an identity number for life, of which the first two digits reflected race (e.g., 00 for white South African). The classification determined the level of rights, including, in the case of indigenous Africans, the binding limitation

Table 3: Racial classifications in the Union/Republic of South Africa, 1911–1996[a]

Year	African	Asian	Coloured	European/White
1911	Bantu[b]		Mixed and other coloured[c]	European/White
1918d				European/White
1921	Natives (Bantu)	Asiatic	Mixed and other coloured	European
1926[d]				Europeans
1931[d]				European
1936	Natives	Asiatics	Coloured	Europeans
1941[d]				European
1946	Natives (Bantu)	Asiatic	Mixed and other coloured	European (White)
1951	Natives	Asiatics	Coloureds	Whites
1960	Bantu	Asiatics	Coloureds	Whites
1970	Bantu	Asiatics	Coloureds	Whites
1980	Blacks	Asians	Coloureds	Whites
1985[e]	Blacks	Asians	Coloureds	Whites
1991	Blacks	Asians	Coloureds	Whites
1996	African/Black	Indian/Asian	Coloured	White

Sources: Official Census Reports and Questionnaires.
Notes:
[a] South Africa became a Republic in 1961.
[b] The Bantu classification consisted of the following subclassifications: Baca, Bachuana, Basuto, Bavenda, Bomvana, Damara, Fingo, Hlangweni, Daffir (unspecified), Ndebele, Northern Rhodesian Tribes, Nyasaland Protectorate Tribes, Other Tribes, Pondo, Pondomise, Portuguese East African Tribes, Southern Rhodesian Tribes, Swazi, Tembu, Tonga (alias for Bagwamba including Tshangana), Xesibe, Xosa and Zulu.
[c] The Mixed and Coloured other than Bantu classification consisted of the following subclassifications: Afghan, American Coloured, Arabian, Bushman, Chinese, Creole, Egyptian, Griqua, Hottentot, Indian, Koranna-'Hottentot Races', Krooman, Malagasy, Malay (Cape), Mauritian, Mixed, Mozambique, Namaqa-'Hottentot Races', Other, St. Helena, Syrian, West Indian and Zanzibari.
[d] Census of the European population only.
[e] Household census only.

that a reference book proving the right to be or work in certain areas had to be carried at all times on penalty of imprisonment.

The apartheid state provides, therefore, what may be

the clearest example of an illegitimate state, in which being *un*counted could be an exercise in power for marginalized groups – rather than seeking inclusion in statistics that may elsewhere determine allocations of power or resources. In fact, South African census data were used as the basis of allocation decisions for the deployment of military forces. The end of apartheid in 1994 offers a unique statistical anecdote on the question of groups' will to be counted.

As Khalfani and Zuberi explain, the last apartheid census in 1991 was a failure. The African National Congress had demanded a delay, and media coverage questioned why racial identification was necessary in the survey if the Population Registration Act was to repealed, as had been announced. In the end, only 64 per cent of the population – and 54 per cent of the African population – was included.

With the end of the apartheid and the election of Nelson Mandela in 1994 as president of a government of national unity, the 1996 census was a dramatically different exercise. For the first time, South Africans of all races would be counted by a democratically elected government. As Table 4 shows, the resulting level of enumeration was also dramatically different. All groups saw a reversal of the 1991 undercount, with 'European' and 'Asian' groups going back to (apartheid) historical levels. 'African' undercounting, which had risen from around 20 per cent historically to over 40 per cent in 1991, fell to just 10 per cent.

Table 4: Estimated undercount by race (%) and year

Race	1980[a]	1985[a]	1991[a]	1996
African	22.00	20.40	46.20	10.50
Coloured	3.20	3.50	12.40	10.50
European	8.50	5.50	10.80	9.00
Asian	4.40	6.50	15.40	6.10

Source: Akil Khalfani and Tukufu Zuberi, 2001, 'Racial classification and the modern census in South Africa, 1911–1996', *Race and Society* 4, table 5, derived from official statistics.
Notes: All numbers are rounded. The estimates of undercount for 1980, 1985 and 1991 do not include TBVC areas (Transkei, Bophuthatswana, Venda and Ciskei).

Perceived state legitimacy is clearly important for census participation, just as it is for tax compliance.[20] Earlier experiences of post-independence census-taking showed the same issues in a harsh light. To return to Ghana, the 1960 census of the newly independent state was characterized by a very deliberate effort to recover the role of counting. Of Kwame Nkrumah's largely successful efforts, Gerardo Serra writes:

> [I]n order for the census to act as a political technology capable of accurately quantifying the state's *potential* wealth in people (in the form of accurate numbers) and actualizing it (in the form of political support), the education campaign had to inscribe the count within the narrative of a new social contract. This narrative revolved around exchanging people's cooperation with the promise of material progress, thus removing the census from the semantic spheres of taxation and surveillance that had hindered the colonial regime's capacity to provide an accurate population count.[21]

As chapter 5 explores, taxation can play an important role in strengthening the social contract. But the legacy of illegitimate states is inevitably one of distrust, and often one of extractive rather than inclusive taxation. Looking beyond explicitly discriminatory states and census enumeration, a range of systematically uncounted groups can be seen in the most basic government data – that on birth and death.

Life and Death, Uncounted

> I have no accurate knowledge of my age, never having seen any authentic record containing it. By far the larger part of the slaves know as little of their ages as horses know of theirs, and it is the wish of most masters within my knowledge to keep their slaves thus ignorant. I do not remember to have ever met a slave who could tell of his birthday. They seldom come nearer to it than planting-time, harvest-time,

cherry-time, spring-time, or fall-time. A want of information concerning my own was a source of unhappiness to me even during childhood. The white children could tell their ages. I could not tell why I ought to be deprived of the same privilege.

Frederick Douglass[22]

Census data rests on two further aspects of the 'Leave no one behind' agenda: vital registration, and legal identity. Target 16.9 of the SDGs reads: 'By 2030, provide legal identity for all, including birth registration.'

Overall, despite some improvement over the last decade, there is no birth registration for around one-third of children under the age of 5, and more than 100 countries lack functioning systems for registration.[23] My former colleagues at the Center for Global Development, Casey Dunning, Alan Gelb and Sneha Raghavan, argued for such a target in the SDGs, highlighting three reasons for which this type of counting is crucial: first, that recognized identity supports the establishment of (at least notional) rights vis-à-vis a state; second, that it facilitates (practical) access to state services; and third, to support better data. Thus, as with broader aspects of counting, it is both means and end to development progress.

And as ever, the uncounted here are not an arbitrary group. Dunning et al. write: '[I]t is no accident that those lacking birth registration and legal identity are typically the most vulnerable people in the poorest countries.' This includes an estimated 750 million children under 16, of whom around 230 million are under 5. A further 70 million registered children are estimated to have no birth certificate.[24]

Analysis using household survey data takes this analysis further. Researchers from the International Center for Equity in Health examined data for 94 countries, covering more than 4 million children.[25] In 29 countries, more than 90 per cent of children had birth certificates. In 36 countries, the figure was below half of all children.

Across the sample, children from rural areas and those from lower-wealth households were systematically less likely to be registered – but at the same time, the presence of (lower-income) countries with near universal coverage demonstrate the feasibility of such a target. Similarly, UNICEF has shown that registration is least likely for children born into poorer households and to mothers with lower levels of education; and in some countries, to certain ethnolinguistic and/or religious groups.[26] Wendy Hunter of the University of Texas has examined cases around the world, highlighting in particular the exclusion of indigenous and Afro-descendant populations in Latin America, and certain groups elsewhere, including, for example, Nubian and Somali people in Kenya, Kurds in Turkey, and non-Lao peoples in Vietnam.[27]

Hunter also evaluates an important critique of the likely benefits of registration – specifically, that it rests on three assumptions:

> that state services, opportunities, benefits, and protections actually exist to obtain; that their access is strictly dependent on the possession of a birth certificate or other formal document and that alternatives are not accepted; [and] that there are no other more fundamental economic, political, or social obstacles to accessing benefits and services.[28]

Hunter shows the significant growth of public services, including cash transfer schemes, around the world, and the extent to which formal identification has indeed become increasingly a requirement for access. On the last point, Hunter argues that while registration is not always the binding constraint, it often is – so the critique does not amount to a justification not to address registration as a priority.

A further set of concerns relate to the linkages between legal identity and citizenship.[29] These include the general risk that attention to legal identity exacerbates the problems faced by those who are stateless (e.g., that they may receive an identity that confers illegal status, in effect; or that the SDGs' emphasis on accountability to citizens may exclude them more comprehensively even than is currently the case). The need to ensure rights *regardless of* legal identity or citizenship is not made generally explicit (although migrants are explicitly included in some targets) – and it should be.

Registration of deaths is less salient in development discussions, perhaps because of a reasonable focus on the rights of the living. But the failure to count deaths is both indicative of deeper inequalities, and also inherently damaging because a blindness to systematic inequalities will prevent moves to address them.

Recent years have seen media organizations focus on compiling statistics to draw attention to important uncounted mortality. These relate both to people who are so marginalized that official statistics do not note their passing; and to people whose mortality occurs at the hands of more powerful actors who have chosen not to record it.

In the latter group, consider the victims of US police shootings and other killings. For nearly ten years until March 2014, the US Bureau of Justice Statistics tried to gather data on 'arrest-related deaths'. They gave up, citing a lack of participation by police departments, including some of the biggest like the NYPD. A year later, in March 2015, the *Guardian* launched its own effort to compile a count.[30] Six months after that, then FBI head James Comey told a high-level summit of US law enforcement and politicians that it was 'unacceptable', 'ridiculous – and embarrassing' that the *Guardian* and *Washington Post* had better data on this.

A further year later, in December 2016, the Bureau of Justice Statistics published preliminary findings of a pilot programme aiming to combine police force reporting with open source data such as the *Guardian*'s project.[31] Sadly, as at March 2019, there has been no further official publication.[32]

Marginalized groups too are often uncounted in high-income countries. In the UK, many local authorities either do not produce statistics on the deaths of homeless people, or else demonstrably underreport deaths. The Bureau of Investigative Journalism (TBIJ) has produced UK statistics, establishing a reporting hub for local journalists to participate – including as a partner in Scotland, The Ferret.[33] Now both National Records of Scotland and the UK Office for National Statistics (ONS) have confirmed they are reviewing their approaches, and that the ONS will soon publish experimental statistics.[34]

Migrants as a group are often marginalized because of their uncertain status, and are often vulnerable in their attempts to reach other countries. Migration to the European Union has met a brutal political climate, with predictable – and predictably uncounted – results. A 2015 study by Reem Abu-Hayyeh and Frances Webber for the UK's Institute of Race Relations, 'Unwanted, unnoticed: an audit of 160 asylum and immigration-related deaths in Europe', provided a snapshot of both the terrible set of outcomes, and the failure to count or qualify deaths in most European countries. Of the 123 deaths the authors attribute to immigration and asylum-related causes, suicide accounted for nearly half. The rest reflected a combination of medical factors including untreated conditions and the denial or severe delay of medical assistance, police and other homicide, accidents, deaths during escape attempts and after deportation. More than 30 cases studied could not be attributed to a particular cause; and 63 who died in Norway, Ireland, France, Germany and the UK could not even be identified. 'In such cases, the dead are in a very literal sense "unmournable".'[35]

The *Guardian* has worked here also, establishing a project called The List, together with the Dutch NGO, United for Intercultural Action, London's Chisenhale Gallery and the Liverpool Biennial.[36] This is an effort simply to count the total number of migrant deaths: at sea, in detention centres and in the communities where they had hoped to build a new life. As at June 2018, The List stood at 34,361.

Perhaps homeless people and migrants seem highly marginal, and their uncounted deaths less surprising. What about women? It turns out the US hasn't had for a decade an official maternal mortality rate, because of concerns over the quality and lack of consistency in the data being reported by different authorities. But a global study for *The Lancet* found that the US stands out as the only high-income country where the rate had risen during the MDG period (1990–2015), to 26.4 deaths per 100,000 live births, compared to fewer than 10 deaths in the likes of the UK, France and Spain, and fewer than 5 in Ireland, Italy, Denmark and Finland.[37]

It may be that being an outlier in not counting these deaths is entirely unrelated to being an outlier in failing to reduce deaths. It may be that the poor quality of all the underlying data means the estimates for the US are completely wrong. The fact that nobody could tell with any certainty for such a long period is, however, inarguable – and inarguably reflects the marginalization of women. The data that does exist confirms a further layer to that marginalization: black women in the US suffered a rate of pregnancy-related mortality more than three times higher than that for white women.[38]

A recent controversy in the US on uncounted mortality, which received somewhat more attention, relates to the death toll from Hurricane Maria, which devastated Puerto Rico in September 2017. Mortality matters additionally in this case because the extent of federal government support after natural disasters will tend to reflect the perceived scale. Shortly after the hurricane, officials put the death toll at 64 – but people in Puerto Rico, as well as external independent researchers and the media, estimated much, much higher figures.[39] In June 2018, the government of Puerto Rico published a comprehensive estimate, showing that 1,427 people were likely to have died, in excess of what would have been expected without the hurricane.[40]

Internationally, mortality statistics become a trigger for action in a more direct sense in the context of whether or not famine should be declared. The Integrated Food Security and Humanitarian Phase Classification Framework (IPC) was introduced in the 2000s as a standard way to categorize situations based on objective data – to take the politics out of famine declaration, as far as possible. The IPC has five phases of food insecurity, of which the final level equates to an announcement of famine. This requires data to demonstrate that 20 per cent of households face extreme food shortages; more than 30 per cent of children under 5 suffer from acute malnutrition (measured by weight and height); and at least two out of every 10,000 people are dying every day.

The conflict in Yemen which began in 2015 has morphed from civil war into a proxy war between regional and international powers, causing widespread harm and vulnerability, including grave food insecurity. A declaration of famine would be highly sensitive politically, for various reasons. It would confirm the view of the Houthi rebels that the coalition backing the internationally recognized government was responsible for great suffering; and also that the aid delivered by donor countries (many supporting the coalition) had failed sufficiently to mitigate the human costs. A declaration of famine could also lead to pressure for UN sanctions against those backing either or both sides.

In such a situation, data is difficult to obtain because of the inherent challenges of conflict; difficult to obtain because of the interests of some parties in avoiding a particular finding; and difficult to evaluate fairly, given the various interests in distorting the data and/or its subsequent interpretation. Within the IPC framework, a final evaluation is made by experts with a chair from the relevant government (although it is unclear how a situation with competing governing parties would be resolved).

Data on mortality rates – the third criterion – are especially problematic. UN Yemen head Lise Grande said: 'Given the complete breakdown in the health system, and the total inability to realistically collect mortality figures, we will almost certainly never know concretely what is going on with the mortality indicator' – raising the possibility that regardless of the reality, it might never be possible to declare a famine. Famine expert Alex de Waal has noted that a million people could die without a declaration, but argues that the system is still useful – at least, 'the best we have for now'.[41]

By setting an objectively verifiable standard, the IPC has displaced some of the politics from the decision itself and onto the data – a step forward, without eliminating the obstacle. The December 2018/January 2019 evaluation of Yemen by the IPC found that 15.9 million people (53 per cent of the population analysed) are severely food insecure, including 36 per cent (about 10.8 million people) in Phase 3 ('Crisis'); 17 per cent of the population (about 5 million people) in Phase 4 ('Emergency'); and 63,500 people in Phase 5 ('Catastrophe', or famine).

Uncount*able?*

The UK has often prided itself on having a National Health Service (NHS) that is envied around the world, and also on the quality of health data and associated standards of research and innovation. With respect to maternal mortality, the World Health Organisation (WHO) states: 'The UK Confidential Enquiry into Maternal Deaths (CEMD) is the longest running system for maternal death review and the methodology is regarded as the global standard.'[42] The *British Journal of Anaesthesia* wrote in a 2005 op-ed: 'The Report on Confidential Enquiries into Maternal Deaths has been a remarkable success. It has saved the lives of countless mothers over the past 50 years.'[43]

But the label of learning disability is now the equivalent, in the UK, of being diagnosed with a life-limiting illness – and still there is no systematic collection of data, no national review process to understand why and no policy package to address the causes. The Learning Disabilities

Mortality Review's (LeDeR) Annual Report 2016–2017 summarizes a programme run by the University of Bristol on behalf of NHS England, which aims to collate and review the deaths of people with learning disabilities.[44] The report recognizes issues of timeliness due to lack of capacity, lack of training, reviewers having other duties, and – underpinning all of these – that the programme itself has not been formally mandated.

The results show that the median age at death of women with learning disabilities (from the age of 4) was 56 years; and for men, 59 years. For the general population of the UK, life expectancy for 2014–16 was 86 and 82 for women and men, respectively – suggesting that living with learning disabilities in one of the richest countries in the world may rob you of the best part of 30 years of life.[45] Those figures represent a sharp deterioration even from 2010–12, when the government's Confidential Inquiry into Premature Deaths of People with Learning Disabilities (CIPOLD, the forerunner of the LeDeR programme) showed the median age of death for women with learning disabilities was 63 years, and for men, 65 years.[46]

The Centre for Welfare Reform showed in 2015 that 29 per cent of the cuts imposed under the government's 'austerity' programme had been borne by just 8 per cent of the population: people living with disabilities.[47] Did that cost people with learning disabilities seven years of their lives? Or did the LeDeR counting improve, to show the true, worse picture? This remains an open question, because successive governments of all parties have failed to ensure that there is sufficient data to answer this or many other fundamental questions about living with learning disabilities in the UK. In 2013, CIPOLD called for the establishment of a National Learning Disability Mortality Review Body. Why? Because lives are saved by systematically collecting, reviewing and learning from mortality data. But the government rejected the recommendation, apparently on the grounds that it would be too expensive.[48]

In 2016, a damning report by the UN Committee on

Economic, Social and Cultural Rights recommended that the UK 'review its policies and programmes introduced since 2010 and conduct a comprehensive assessment of the cumulative impact of these measures on the enjoyment of economic, social and cultural rights by disadvantaged and marginalized individuals and groups, in particular women, children and people living with disabilities, that is recognized by all stakeholders'. The refusal to collect or publish disaggregated data on groups such as people living with disabilities is a running theme of the report.[49]

There's no particular reason I'm aware of to think that the UK establishment is any less interested than their counterparts in any other country, in the lives of people with learning disabilities. And so it is possible that there is no more excluded and marginalized group worldwide than people with learning disabilities. There are certainly much more harshly and deliberately victimized groups in many places – but a single group, neglected to the point of rights abuse on a global basis ...?

It's not useful to speculate about this anyway, and certainly not to set up any group against any other (and in no way is this speculation intended to downplay other global dimensions of exclusion such as gender, caste or indigenous identity). But it strikes me as being at least worth thinking about, because the idea can't be – or shouldn't be – dismissed immediately as ludicrous.

You might then ask yourself how it could be that the underlying conditions to accept such a pattern of rights abuse can exist, systematically, across all sorts of societies with all sorts of histories and at all sorts of per capita income levels; and whether the exclusion of people with learning disabilities globally has anything like the level of public awareness, attention or outrage that it should have.

At the global level, counting appears to be worse. The most recent reference is the WHO/World Bank *World Report on Disability* – which dates back to 2011. The online introductory text reads: 'About 15% of the world's population lives with some form of disability, of whom

2–4% experience significant difficulties in functioning. The global disability prevalence is higher than previous WHO estimates, which date from the 1970s and suggested a figure of around 10%.' And so the statistics I quoted earlier are, at best, eight years out of date, and also represent what seems likely to be only the second ever global estimate – certainly only the second of the last half-century.

We could print a blank page here, to show all the results you find if you search 'disability', to say nothing of 'learning disability', in UN and World Bank data portals. Uncounted, invisibly. Or alternatively we could reprint Recommendation 8 (out of 9) from the *World Report on Disability* and its very sensible and completely unfulfilled call to '[i]mprove disability data collection'. You can imagine the sort of thing: 'Data needs to be dis-aggregated by population features, such as age, sex, race and socioeconomic status, to uncover patterns, trends and information about subgroups of persons with disabilities.' And so on.

As an antidote to pessimism, there are bright spots to be found. Stonewall published a report on LGBT health in the UK, based on a major survey. While the statistics on LGBT people with disabilities are consistently more negative in terms of physical and mental health outcomes, it is vital for any hope of progress to see the questions asked and the extent of intersectional issues revealed.[50] When there is a desire to address marginalization, starting with the right people asking the questions – nothing about us, without us – the challenges of counting do not seem so insurmountable.

The Justice for LB campaign, coming out of the completely unnecessary death of 18-year-old Connor Sparrowhawk while in 'care' in the UK, has developed into a grassroots movement of people living with disabilities and their families. (Full disclosure: Connor lived across the road from me and I love these guys.) The 'LB Bill', which has been discussed in the UK Parliament, could yet change the law – and the counting – forever.[51]

Disenfranchised

People living with disabilities are also disproportionately likely to lack identification documents. In the US, where photo ID requirements for voting have proliferated, this means that people with disabilities are also more likely to be excluded.[52]

There are two ways to stop people exerting political power in a nominal democracy. One is to exclude them by law from voting, as under apartheid. Such a blunt approach is likely to raise eyebrows in polite circles these days, however, so a slightly more subtle version is to introduce laws that limit voting – in the knowledge that they will have systematic effects on certain groups. If you know there is a major racist bias in your criminal justice system, for example, you might increase its impact on voting patterns by disenfranchising felons. The Florida ballot held with the US 2018 midterm elections finally removed this law there, and at a stroke restored the voting rights of around 1.4 million people. But the law remains in place in many other states.

Or if marginalized rural populations are unlikely to support you – say Bedouins in the Negev,[53] or Hispanic Americans in Dodge City, Kansas[54] – you might just make sure there are no polling stations for miles.

The other way is to make it harder for certain groups to vote, to limit their overall influence but without excluding them completely as a group. So introducing photo ID requirements will change average voting propensities. Allowing a gun permit to meet the requirement, as in Texas, but not – say – a student ID, will go further. Making it harder to register on election day will also help. Carol Anderson of Emory University has shown how you can combine these games, by requiring ID but making it much harder for certain communities to obtain the necessary paperwork because of the location of the relevant offices (as, e.g., in Georgia).[55] In North Dakota, ID laws currently require a residential address – effectively disenfranchising around 5,000 Native Americans whose ID gives a PO Box instead.[56]

Millions of people have been purged from US voter rolls too. In Georgia (again), this was done on the basis of people having not voted in recent elections, or not confirming an address – both likely to affect those on lower incomes and, in this case, black and ethnic minority people. In June 2018, the Supreme Court voted 5–4 to allow the purging of those who hadn't voted in recent elections – allowing states to pursue the exclusion of a subset of people who will in almost all cases be disproportionately lower-income and from minority groups.[57]

Ari Berman of Mother Jones, who has long reported and campaigned on US voter suppression, points the finger at the 2013 Supreme Court ruling that undermined the Voting Rights Act, and allowed states with a long history of voting discrimination to make changes to their voting rules without federal approval.[58] The same dynamics of uncounting that apply in many other areas exist in voting too – the only difference here is that the suppression can be more open, and more deliberate. But think of the continuing revelations of opaque funding for recent elections around the world, including the Brexit referendum in the UK; and the often closely related abuses of access to personal data, often with the aim of targeted social media messaging to suppress voting.

The US census carried out every decade is the basis for determining the numbers of congressional seats and electoral votes that states receive, and also for the allocation of $880 billion in federal funding between states and localities.[59] This chapter began with a quote from the US Constitution, showing the decision to apportion political representatives on the basis of 'adding to the whole Number of free Persons, including those bound to Service for a Term of Years, and excluding Indians not taxed, three fifths of all other Persons'. Legal constraints may, in these enlightened times, prevent explicit allocation of lower weight to certain groups of people. But in practice the scope for manipulation is great – and, at the time of writing, the US has a presidential administration that is very keen to exploit it.

Post-enumeration surveys suggest that the 2010 census may have been the most accurate of recent times – and potentially the most accurate ever. While the 2000 survey showed an overcount of around 0.5 per cent in total, 1990 and 1980 saw undercounts of nearer 1.5 per cent. The 2010 census showed an overcount of 0.01 per cent, not statistically different from zero.

The 2010 census still had significant underlying inequalities though. Some reflect consistent problems of counting – people in 'group' accommodation like student dormitories rather than households, and renters as against homeowners, for example. Others reflect not the power associated with these living characteristics, but the power associated with ethnolinguistic groups.

Non-Hispanic white people were overcounted by 0.8 per cent in 2010. In contrast, 1.5 per cent of Hispanic people and 2.1 per cent of black people went uncounted. For Asian people (uncounted by 0.1 per cent), and the 'Native Hawaiian and Other Pacific Islander' (1.3 per cent), the uncounting was not statistically different from zero. The most highly excluded group was that of 'American Indians and Alaska Natives living on reservations', of whom 4.9 per cent went uncounted.[60]

The effects of such uncounting – even in a relatively good year – are very substantial. The estimated 1.5 million people uncounted in California will have cost the state $1.7 billion in annual federal funding, and one or more congressional districts.[61] Money and power, lost in the data.

At the aggregate level, average voting patterns mean that the ethnolinguistic groups most likely to go uncounted are those that tend to deliver consistently higher support for Democrat politicians than for Republicans (whose core white voters are overcounted). That pattern has strengthened further with the increasingly open racism of the Trump administration, making the incentive to manipulate the count all the stronger.

So far, 2020 census manipulation has taken two main paths. The less direct path has been through the creation of a climate of fear. While not necessarily aimed primarily at achieving a census effect, there is no question that it will. Results of pretesting with potentially vulnerable groups presented by Census Bureau staff in late 2017 showed dramatic impacts of the political context, even early in the Trump administration.[62]

Typical comments included: 'The possibility that the census could give my information to internal security and immigration could come and arrest me for not having documents terrifies me' (from an interview carried out in Spanish); and 'In light of the current political situation, the immigrants, especially the Arabs and Mexicans, would be so scared when they see a government interviewer at their doorsteps' (from a focus group conducted in Arabic). An interviewer fed back that 'in the recent several months before anything begins, I'm being asked times over, does it make a difference if I'm not a citizen?'

The associated counting was powerfully undermined. Unlike in the census itself, pretesting respondents were paid a cash incentive and were recruited through trusted community organizations, and the confidentiality of responses was explained while obtaining informed consent. But even in this favourable context, three behaviours of respondents were consistently noted: nervousness, including requiring detailed information about data redaction and data access; the intentional provision of inaccurate or incomplete information about household members; and seeking to end interviews.

The Census Bureau summarized its findings as 'an unprecedented groundswell in confidentiality and data sharing concerns, particularly among immigrants and those who live with immigrants, [which] may present a barrier to participation [and] could impact data quality and coverage in the 2020 Census [and is] particularly troubling due to the disproportionate impact on hard-to-count populations'.

The more direct path also taken by the Trump administration is an attempt to manipulate the census count by changing the content: to influence who answers by changing what is asked. The Trump administration has reintroduced a question not seen since the 1950 census, asking respondents whether or not they are citizens of the United States.

The immediate effect would be chilling. By comparing and cross-referencing responses from the 2010 census and the 2010 American Community Survey (ACS), which does include a citizenship question, the Census Bureau's Chief Scientist John Abowd was able to lay out evidence on the likely impact.[63] Both 'citizen households' and those containing at least one non-citizen had higher non-response rates for the ACS than for the census. But overall, the drop in response for non-citizen households was 5.1 percentage points higher.

Table 5 summarizes some of the key findings from a more detailed analysis of the most recent ACS surveys, which are likely to reflect more accurately the political context. Two clear points emerge from the responses to the citizenship question, and from the extent of breakoff rates (non-completion of the survey, and when it occurred). First, overall breakoff rates are 1.5–1.9 times higher for Hispanic and non-Hispanic non-white respondents than they are for non-Hispanic white respondents. Breakoffs tracked specifically to the point at which respondents see citizenship questions show relative ratios that are much higher.

Second, non-response rates on the citizenship question are twice as high for Hispanic and non-Hispanic black respondents as they are for non-Hispanic white respondents. That divergence grew, comparing internet-based responses in 2016 to those in 2013 for Hispanic and non-Hispanic black respondents, but was unchanged for non-Hispanic white respondents.

Table 5: Deterrent impact of citizenship questions, American Community Survey (%)

	Non-Hispanic white	Non-Hispanic black	Hispanic
Non-response rates to citizenship question			
Mail-in questionnaire, 2013–16	6.0–6.3	12.0–12.6	11.6–12.3
Internet, 2013	6.2	12.3	13.0
Internet, 2016	6.2	13.1	15.5

	Non-Hispanic white	Non-Hispanic non-white	Hispanic
Breakoff rates at citizenship question	0.04	0.27	0.36
Breakoff rates on any of three citizenship-related questions	0.5	1.2	1.6
Overall breakoff rates	9.5	14.1	17.6

Source: Compiled from John Abowd, 19 January 2018, 'Technical review of the Department of Justice request to add citizenship question to the 2020 census', *Memorandum for Wilbur L. Ross, Jr, Secretary of Commerce.*

Taken together, the Chief Scientist's memo leaves no room for doubt that the effects of including a citizenship question would be to raise substantially the numbers of people uncounted in the 2020 census, with disproportionate impact on already relatively marginalized groups, including non-citizens. Given the role of the census, this uncounting would have substantial macro-level effects in reducing the allocation of both federal funds and political influence for areas in which those groups are most represented.

Having received this evidence, the Secretary of Commerce, Wilbur Ross, gave his decision to go ahead – leaving little question as to the administration's desire, or at least complete indifference, to the discriminatory impact. This open attempt to manipulate the census has at least been the subject of media scrutiny, vigorous political objection, including by the House Committee on Oversight and

Reform, and legal challenge by multiple states' attorneys general. In June 2019, the Supreme Court ruled against the inclusion of the citizenship question. At the time of writing, the administration's response remained unclear.

Already, the sharp cuts to funding of the Census Bureau have resulted in the cancellation of all the 2017 'dress rehearsals' (which were intended to be held in Puerto Rico and on Native American reservations), and two of three of the 2018 rehearsals (including one scheduled for an area with a significant Hispanic population).[64]

And let nobody think that a botched 2020 census could be fixed by an incoming Democrat administration. After the 1990 census uncounted something in the region of 10 million people, the Bureau proposed applying statistical adjustments to the 2000 data in order to make it more accurate – and necessarily including substantial numbers of uncounted, marginalized groups. The Republican then-Speaker of Congress, Newt Gingrich, challenged the proposal, eventually winning a Supreme Court decision to prevent such sampling approaches – and effectively ensuring that the uncounted can only be addressed by improving the raw census data. Which is the opposite of what will happen in 2020.

Census counts in both China (towards 1.4 billion people, 2010 census) and India (1.2 billion people, 2011) are of substantially greater scale, with four or more times the number of people counted in the US. And deliberate uncounting has taken more blatant forms in other states in other periods. But the US census underpins directly the allocation of the best part of a trillion dollars, and also lays the basis for the electoral decisions of what remains the most influential country in the world.

The deliberate manipulation of the 2020 US census is on course to be the most significant single piece of uncounting of our times – and, at the very least, of this century to date. The remaining strength of institutions may prove sufficient to prevent the citizenship question. But unless there is a much more dramatic reversal of political power, the climate of fear that has been created will do most of the damage on its own.

Uncounted at the Bottom

The same important truth holds across all the areas of uncounting we have touched on in Part I of this book: it is a phenomenon that stems from, as well as exacerbating, imbalances of power. At the most blatant, we find governments seeking to suppress data on people they are deliberately marginalizing and excluding from the benefits of a functioning state – from the Bashir regime's efforts to hide a policy of regional supremacy in Sudan, to the Trump administration's attempts to tilt both the allocation of state resources and the future electoral balance towards white Republicans.

We find consistent flaws in the data that must bear the weight of both national and global efforts to promote human progress, including the UN SDGs. Time and again, marginalized groups are uncounted or undercounted – and shown to be disproportionately in poverty where the data do exist. Development's data problem is political, not technical. Technical responses alone will not provide solutions unless they challenge those imbalances.

The uncounted at the bottom are excluded, to greater or less extent, from the benefits of the social contract. Their rights to political representation are curtailed. Their rights to basic services, including access to the rule of law, are undermined. Their political salience, and with it their prospects for greater inclusion, is weakened too.

Nor is this exclusion neutral, or passive. With varying degrees of consciousness, the uncounting of marginalized groups by omission or by commission is willed by people with power. Sometimes, the simple act of holding up a mirror to those actions may be enough to force change. But sometimes, the uncounting will be but a piece of a larger, more deliberate exclusion – say, through racist or supremacist ideology or simple desire to maintain dispro-portionate power.

Power concedes nothing willingly. But the more we open our eyes to what is uncounted, the more likely we are to be able to challenge the political power behind.

Part II

Uncounted and Illicit: The Unmoney Hiding at the Top

The proposed settlor [client] is a Brazilian national, but has been living in Canada for the last 15 years where he considers his permanent home to be. The trustees are to be a trust institution in the Cayman Islands with a professional protector situated in the Bahamas. It is intended that the trust assets will comprise shares in two underlying companies: the holding company of the settlor's Latin American business empire is incorporated as an exempt company in Bermuda; and an IBC [international business corporation] incorporated in [the British Virgin Islands] holding a portfolio of stocks and shares. The discretionary beneficiaries comprise a class of persons who reside throughout Europe and South America.

Client scenario, STEP training manual, quoted by
Brooke Harrington[1]

There's no such thing as good money or bad money. There's just money.

Lucky Luciano[2]

Our assessment [of the IMF's Balance of Payments (BOP) Statistics] paints a less rosy picture: reported figures are far less accurate than they are typically imagined to be and often do not correspond to the theoretical concepts with which users associate them. At the same time, measurement quality deteriorates over time as the transnationalization of economic production gradually undermines the validity of BOP statistics. Our findings raise serious questions about the widespread use of these numbers, with their deceptive pretense to accuracy, in scholarly research and public debate about the international political economy.

Lukas Linsi and Daniel Mügge[3]

4
Uncounted at the Top

This chapter shows how the systemic, global provision of financial secrecy provides rich and already powerful individuals and companies with the opportunity to step out of the laws and expectations of the countries in which they operate, to go uncounted for the purposes of social and legal compliance; and how that distorts even the most basic of economic statistics.

Underpinning every major case of corruption around the world, and many major cases of tax abuse, can be found anonymously owned companies and trusts, from the British Virgin Islands to Delaware; opaque corporate accounting, typically in the biggest stock markets in the world, that obscures the degree of profit shifting and tax avoidance; and deliberate failures to exchange financial information, in order to hide bank accounts.

This deliberately engineered secrecy is not a marginal activity. It stands at the heart of the global economic and financial system. It is embedded in our international trade, investment and banking, like a stick of rock with the word 'Uncounted' running through it. And this aspect of the uncounted is a pernicious threat to any hopes of sustainable progress towards better lives.

There are three main elements to this threat. First, and most easily apparent, the failure to count at the top of distributions results in major losses in tax revenue. Governments are deprived of the very funds needed to support better lives for their people.

The second element is more gradual, but perhaps also more powerful in the end. Non-compliance of the most high-profile actors is corrosive, as others reconsider their own approach. The social contract, the state–citizen relationship and, ultimately, the legitimacy of government are all undermined. As corruption prospers, political representation and governance are weakened. Government actions, including the use of revenues raised, become increasingly unlikely to target, or to deliver, inclusive benefits for the population.

Last and not least, acceptance of the uncounted at the top condemns societies to ignorance about the extent of their own true inequalities. Thomas Piketty has written about France's land registry as an important legacy of the 1789 Revolution. The registry ensured ongoing public and policymaker awareness of land inequality (which at that time was, in effect, wealth inequality). It also provided the means to taxation if and when this was desired. Just as in the case of Sudan's Black Book, the registry challenged the engineered ignorance of inequality that can dissipate pressure for meaningful redistribution.

While Part I of this book dealt mainly with those who are uncounted for the purposes of 'who decides', and 'what people get', Part II focuses on those who are uncounted for the purpose of 'what people are required to do'. A central aspect is the exploitation of different jurisdictions, 'offshore'. There is no shortage of stories, and no lack of variation: from multinationals shifting profits around the world to obscured monopoly positions and political conflicts of interest, to the laundering of the proceeds of crime, including the outright theft of state assets. The consistent feature is that the financial secrecy involved allows circumvention of processes that, for everyone else, are simply a necessary element of being part of a society. Choosing to go uncounted is, in the most literal sense, antisocial.

April 2016. The International Consortium of Investigative Journalists (ICIJ) launches its biggest leak to that point: 11.5 million files from a Panamanian law firm. The leak contains details of the actual owners and controllers of thousands of anonymously owned companies, set up by the firm for its clients over decades in jurisdictions all around the world. One of the first stories to break is that Iceland's prime minister, Sigmundur Davíð Gunnlaugsson, has failed to disclose a major conflict of interest.

After the global financial crisis of 2008, which revealed a series of shocking banking scandals, Gunnlaugsson led a group that campaigned for the country to reject any bailout for foreign creditors of Icelandic financial institutions. Following successful referendums organized by the group InDefence, Gunnlaugsson entered parliament with a mandate to clean up, and, after becoming prime minister in 2013, he led a government whose responsibilities included the negotiation of final terms of payments for the banks' creditors. The deal delivered in 2015 was criticized by InDefence as being too generous.

The Panama Papers revealed that Gunnlaugsson had, with his wife, owned an anonymous company that held millions of dollars worth of bonds in those same banks. Two days later, despite attempts to clarify the actual ownership as being entirely his wife's, Gunnlaugsson resigned.

February 2012. The Rangers Football Club, incorporated as a company in 1899, goes into administration – to be followed, in October 2012, by entering liquidation. One of Scotland's biggest teams, featuring frequently in European competitions, Rangers had begun at the turn of the century a series of increasingly ill-advised tax schemes. By paying senior staff, including international star players, through trusts established in the UK Crown Dependency of Jersey, and with the payments presented as loans rather than income, the club sought to avoid major tax liabilities of tens of millions of pounds (back when that was a lot of money in football).

In this way, Rangers was able to outbid its rivals over the course of a decade that brought the club trophy after trophy. When the tax authority finally caught up with the club, it was already struggling from prolonged financial mismanagement and the more austere approach of its banks after the financial crisis. Attempts to reach a deal with creditors failed.

Fans were distraught at the loss of a century-old institution, although a new club was formed and quickly made its way up through the leagues. But fans of other teams continue to seek redress from the football authorities, for the trophies, and lucrative entry to European football, that their own clubs were denied as a result of the tax cheating of the old Rangers.[1]

August 2018. Erstwhile manager for Donald Trump's presidential campaign, Paul Manafort, is found guilty of multiple counts of tax evasion, after special counsel Robert Mueller presents evidence that

> [Manafort and colleague Rick Gates] funneled millions of dollars in payments [for lobbying work in Ukraine] into foreign nominee companies and bank accounts, opened by them and their accomplices in nominee names and in various foreign countries, including Cyprus, Saint Vincent and the Grenadines (Grenadines), and the Seychelles. Manafort and Gates hid the existence of the foreign companies and bank accounts, falsely and repeatedly reporting to their tax preparers and to the United States that they had no foreign bank accounts.[2]

Classic vanilla tax evasion: no attempts to dress things up, just the straightforward, fraudulent non-declaration of legal entities and bank accounts created in jurisdictions that allow you to do this anonymously. Old school.

March 2008. Bear Stearns, a New York-based, international investment bank becomes the first major casualty of what will turn into the global financial crisis. The market has lost all confidence in the bank and its creditworthiness, due to its exposure to subprime mortgages and other dubious assets.

It subsequently emerges that the bank had major operations through Ireland's International Financial Services Centre. The Dublin holding company had managed to finance $11,900 of assets for every $100 of equity, compared to the international consensus that banks should not exceed $1,250 of risk-weighted assets for each $100 of shareholder capital in order to have a decent cushion against downside risk. The ratio provides a striking indication of the extent to which the 'shadow banking' system was responsible for the enormous growth of credit in the pre-crisis years.

Irish economist James Stewart uncovered the statistics, and also revealed that no regulator had responsibility for Bear Stearns's operations in Dublin. The Irish regulator, the Financial Services Regulatory Authority, appeared to consider itself responsible only for 'Irish banks' – those with headquarters in Ireland. Stewart questions whether *anyone* had ultimate regulatory responsibility for oversight of investment structures of banks headquartered elsewhere, including the US.[3]

Public awareness of Bear Stearns's problems began when the bank was forced to provide billions of dollars to bail out its own subprime hedge funds, in July 2007. In August, the bank's chief economist David Malpass wrote a Panglossian op-ed for the *Wall Street Journal*, 'Don't panic about the credit market': 'the housing- and debt-market corrections will probably add to the length of the U.S. economic expansion.' A few months later, the US was in recession. A few months after that, Bear Stearns was no more. Fun fact: David Malpass is now the head of the World Bank, at Donald Trump's nomination.

May 2013. Apple's chief executive Tim Cook faces the US Senate Permanent Subcommittee on Investigations, which has published evidence that Apple used Irish subsidiaries to dodge tens of billions of dollars of tax. As Simon

Bowers of the ICIJ would subsequently report, Cook defended the company staunchly: 'We pay all the taxes we owe, every single dollar ... We do not depend on tax gimmicks ... We do not stash money on some Caribbean island.'

But, as the ICIJ revealed in November 2017, when Ireland began to tighten up a few months later, Apple went looking. Their law firm Baker McKenzie sent a question-naire to offshore specialists Appleby, whose offices in the Cayman Islands, the British Virgin Islands, Bermuda, the Isle of Man, Guernsey and Jersey were asked to confirm that 'an Irish company can conduct management activities ... without being subject to taxation in your jurisdiction'.[4] This leak shows as clearly as any the blatant nature of the search for 'offshore' as a space to establish a technical presence, as part of a process to step out of regulatory requirements in the locations where real economic activity takes place.

These stories all point towards the key tools of the secrecy trade. For individuals, it is the availability of anonymous bank accounts and of legal entities that allow anonymous ownership – companies, trusts and founda-tions. For multinationals, it is the absence of requirements for a full accounting in each country of their activities, profits and tax paid.

At the same time, even multiple, compelling stories do not necessarily convey the importance of the issue. If there were only a few bad Apples[5] – a few multinationals, a few people going uncounted at the margins – would it matter? For various reasons, it still would. But in fact, the evidence demonstrates that these pernicious practices are systemic, and of first order importance as purely economic phenomena – even before we consider the governance impact.

Profit Shifting and Undeclared Ownership

Multinational groups are able to shift their taxable profits away from the location of the underlying economic activity, because of the deeply flawed international tax rules over which the Organization for Economic Cooperation and Development (OECD) group of rich countries presides. These rules, following decisions of the League of Nations in the 1920s and 1930s, take an approach called 'separate accounting'. This involves treating each entity within a multinational group as if it is individually profit-maximizing – even though the entire economic logic of multinationals is that they are jointly managed to maximize profit centrally, and exist only where this is more efficient than separate entities carrying out the same business.

The system relies on the arm's length principle, which requires that transactions between companies within the same group be priced as if the companies were not part of the same group but unrelated (that is, operating at arm's length from each other). It is notoriously difficult to verify such prices, even for basic commodities that are openly traded on the free market. For intragroup lending, or payments for access to intangibles including intellectual property which are likely to be group-specific and never traded on the open market, establishing 'arm's length prices' is an exercise in hunting for unicorns.

The OECD recognizes six different methods, which allows enormous latitude to multinationals and their many advisers from the big law and accounting firms to engineer more favourable tax outcomes. As multinational groups have become more complex and powerful over recent decades, the League of Nations' decision has become increasingly outdated – and profit shifting an increasingly large and urgent problem.

In some ways, of course, the model of multinational companies has not changed at all. A cynic might argue that regardless of the laws in place, the approach has always been to take out everything possible from poorer countries at least, and to pay as little as possible for the privilege. That cynic might well point you towards one of the very first multinationals, the East India Company.

Local producers were initially 'paid' for their work in

rupees, out of the state budget – a budget that was in no small part based on taxes levied on those same producers. A later stage used bills of exchange to achieve a not dissimilar result, at least in terms of the East India Company paying very little for export goods – which, like any good multinational, it sold internationally for a much higher price than it had paid. Those exports were responsible for India running among the world's largest trade surpluses, but the gold and silver that others paid for it all ended up in London. The economist Utsa Patnaik recently estimated the total value of this extraction from India between 1765 and 1938 at $45 trillion, or around 15 times the UK's current GDP.[6]

Insulating multinationals and tax authorities from accountability these days, rather than colonial impunity, is the lack of meaningful data. Individual companies operating in single economies can expect to publish their accounts and their ownership. This transparency expectation dates back to the introduction of limited liability, which allows company directors to take entrepreneurial risks without their entire assets – for example, the family home – being put at risk too. This inevitably passes risk somewhere else – it ends up with the company's suppliers, customers and competitors, as well as with the state.

The quid pro quo for capping directors' liability in this way is that companies provide transparency. This means that suppliers, customers and competitors, as well as any member of the public and official bodies such as tax authorities, can have some confidence that limited liability is not being misused – and therefore that the risks being passed on to others by company directors are also to some degree limited.

Broadly, this expected transparency has the effect that anyone can see the extent of a company's activities in the country of operation, as well as their declared profits and tax paid. What multinationals have managed over time, largely through the work of the major accounting firms which exert effective control over largely control international accounting standards, is to lower their own required transparency far below this expectation.

The exertion of multinationals' power to reduce their transparency – and with it, their accountability – has been well documented. Despite decades of efforts by lower-income countries at the UN to establish higher standards, multinationals and their high-income home countries have successfully resisted.[7] And at the same time, the geographic reporting requirements in international accounting standards have been actively weakened or removed.

Through this combination of engineered complexity and engineered opacity, multinational companies have made their tax affairs increasingly uncounted. The effect is seen most clearly in analysis of the aggregate data of US multinationals, published by the Bureau of Economic Analysis. The data lumps together the activity of all US multinationals in each country, so is likely to understate the true distortions, but for the moment this is the best available source of comparative data over time.

To understand the extent of misalignment, Petr Janský and I compared where profits were declared and tax paid with the locations of the multinationals' sales, employment and tangible assets.[8] The analysis shows that in the 1990s, depending on the measure of activity we use, around 5–10 per cent of the global profits in the sample were declared for tax purposes in places other than where the underlying activity took place.

Roll forward to the early 2010s, however, and the picture changes dramatically. Now we find that 25–30 per cent of global profits are misaligned with activity. Our preferred spot estimate for shifted profit in 2012 amounts to $660 billion, 27 per cent of US multinationals' gross profit or approximately 0.9 per cent of world GDP. Other research shows that when multinationals took on one of the big four accounting firms to do their audits, they increased the extent of their tax haven usage – and that there is a causal element, not just correlation, to this finding.[9] The complexity of multinational structures, and the erosion of accounting standards, generated an explosion of profit shifting.

It is this rapid change in the scale of the problem, coupled with the politics of the aftermath of the financial crisis, that led OECD countries – for once feeling the fiscal pressures more familiar to their lower-income counterparts – to seek a comprehensive reform of the international tax rules. The Base Erosion and Profit Shifting initiative (BEPS) ran for two years, from 2013 to 2015, and had just a single goal: to reduce the misalignment between profits and the location of real economic activity.

Multiple studies have now used a range of data sources to estimate the revenue losses associated with profit shifting worldwide. All put the cost at between $100 billion and $600 billion a year. The leading academic estimate finds that 40 per cent of multinationals' profits are artificially shifted to tax havens, with an estimated revenue loss around $200 billion a year, around 10 per cent of global corporate tax revenue. The UN Conference on Trade and Development (UNCTAD) and OECD estimates are close to this range also. Researchers at the IMF put the long-run estimates of revenue loss at $400 billion for OECD countries (1 per cent of their GDP) and $200 billion for lower-income countries (1.3 per cent of their GDP), while Petr Janský and I reran this analysis with stronger tax data and arrived at slightly lower estimates (roughly $300 billion and $200 billion for high- and lower-income countries respectively).[10]

Lower-income countries typically obtain total tax revenues in the range of 15–25 per cent of GDP, and sometimes lower, while OECD countries typically obtain between 30 per cent and 45 per cent. The disparity in losses as a share of current tax revenue demonstrates how much more intense the problem of profit shifting is for many lower-income countries.

At the same time, the research is clear that only a handful of jurisdictions are responsible for imposing most of the losses on all other countries (at all levels of per capita income). For US multinationals, these are the Netherlands, Luxembourg, Bermuda, Cayman, Ireland, Switzerland and Singapore. Others include, to varying degrees, additional UK Overseas Territories such as the British Virgin Islands; UK Crown Dependencies Jersey, Guernsey and the Isle of Man; smaller EU states, including Cyprus, Malta and Belgium; and a handful more from other regions, including Mauritius, the Seychelles and Hong Kong.[11]

Aside from the revenue losses, profit shifting and related manipulations of cross-border investment (real and otherwise) cause significant distortion to basic economic statistics. Studies find non-trivial impacts on the capital share of corporate value added, on the size of trade deficits, and even on GDP, in a range of countries according to whether they attract or lose out from profit shifting – and these are big enough to affect quite well-known economic 'facts':

> For instance, after accounting for profit shifting, Japan, the UK, France, and Greece turn out to have trade surpluses in 2015, in contrast to the published data that record trade deficits. According to our estimates, the true trade deficit of the United States was 2.1% of GDP in 2015, instead of 2.8% in the official statistics – that is, a quarter of the recorded trade deficit of the United States is an illusion of multinational corporate tax avoidance.[12]

Research published by the IMF shows that almost 40 per cent of all foreign direct investment globally is artificial.[13] In effect, some $12 trillion is passing through foreign entities with no economic substance at all. Great swathes of the investment into economies large and small come, on paper, from the tiniest jurisdictions. Much of this is round-tripping, disguised domestic investment – whether to avoid tax or regulation, to hide conflicts of interest or to obtain 'foreign investor' benefits.

Perhaps the most striking example of statistical distortion is the 26 per cent jump in Ireland's GDP in 2015, along with an associated jump of close to $270 billion in capital stock, which is widely believed to reflect a tax-motivated restructuring by Apple, and the possible reallocation of more than $200 billion in intangible assets to one of its Irish subsidiaries.[14] Research has shown, too, how the divergence between Ireland's recorded GDP and its real economic performance masked the stagnant labour market performance as ordinary people saw little or no benefit from the macroeconomic statistical distortions.[15]

Lukas Linsi and Daniel Mügge, political scientists at the University of Amsterdam quoted at the beginning of this Part, have long studied the same phenomena, in the context of distortions to capitalism. Their work at FickleFormulas.org aims to track both the weaknesses of data, often related to profit shifting and financial secrecy behaviours, and also the divergence of the subjective understanding of analysts who use the data. This adds an important further dimension, because to a certain extent issues of mismeasurement can be contained by detailed knowledge and a cautious approach. When instead the users of statistics generally believe any errors to be limited and random, and the quality of data to be improving over time, the risks of careless analysis leading to powerful but erroneous policy conclusions become much greater.

Many of the leading jurisdictions for profit shifting have also been central to the provision of anonymous ownership vehicles, and of anonymous bank accounts – along with some others that specialize on the secrecy side. The two most widely cited estimates of the resulting scale of undeclared ownership have come from James Henry, a senior adviser to the Tax Justice Network and former chief economist for McKinsey's, and from Gabriel Zucman, an economist at Berkeley. Henry's estimate reflects a wide set of asset types and looks across all jurisdictions through which assets are held, and generates a range of $21 trillion to $32 trillion. In contrast, Zucman's estimate is of around $8 trillion of a narrower range of financial assets, held in a predetermined set of 'tax haven' jurisdictions. Both studies estimate an associated revenue loss from the undeclared offshore income stream of around $190 billion annually (Henry assumes a much more cautious rate of his return, on his much higher estimated stock).[16]

The Tax Justice Network published a further study alongside the Henry analysis, called *Inequality: You Don't Know the Half of It (or Why Inequality Is Worse than We Thought)*.[17] Here, the second important effect of this hidden wealth is laid out. The revenue losses are substantial, and in their own right will contribute to greater inequality because the burden of foregone public expenditure on the likes of health and education will be borne disproportionately by lower-income groups. But in addition, there are three further channels that will compound this damage.

First, actual inequality will be higher than is recorded – because official statistics will not capture undeclared wealth and income. This is likely, over time, to be associated with lower pressure for redistribution than if the public and policymakers were fully aware of the true scale of inequality.

Second, the absence of data indicates policy ineffectiveness. Without knowing the true levels of offshore wealth and income, the tax authorities cannot hope to enforce taxation. That undermines the progressiveness of the given set of tax policies, making final inequality higher than would have been the case otherwise.

Third, this will also over time be likely to contribute to a more regressive set of policies. If policymakers can't make direct taxes on income and wealth work, the fiscal pressure will pass to a combination of lower spending and/or more regressive taxation, such as consumption taxes like VAT. In both cases, lower-income groups will bear more of the burden, and the result will be higher inequality.

Overall, the failure to count offshore wealth and income will exert a powerful upward pressure on national inequalities – both recorded and unrecorded.

Gabriel Zucman and collaborators have done much additional work, using the data collected from tax authorities in the World Inequality Database and supporting data from a range of sources, including leaks, to look at the implications for undeclared offshore wealth holdings – and so for inequality at the national level.[18] They find major national variations under the umbrella estimate that about 10 per cent of world GDP is held offshore. At the low end, Scandinavian countries appear to have only a few per cent of GDP offshore. At the high end, the figures can reach up to 60 per cent in some Latin American countries and Russia. Western Europe has values around 15 per cent. A significant finding is that simple geographic proximity to Switzerland is associated with higher offshore wealth. So too are political and economic instability, and natural resource wealth.

These authors also find important variation in the distribution of offshore wealth. In general, however, it is overwhelmingly concentrated at the top end: not the top 10 per cent of households, nor even the top 1 per cent, but the top 0.1 per cent and, above all (never better said), the top 0.01 per cent. In Norway, accounting for offshore wealth increases the top 0.01 per cent's wealth by around 25 per cent. The results suggest, overall, that the decline in European wealth inequality over the last century may have been much smaller than thought.

The fact that even such a well-established finding may be in question shows just how important this aspect of the uncounted could be. What chance can there be that we have the levels of wealth inequality that are politically pre-ferred, or economically 'efficient' if there is such a thing, when we have so little idea what those levels of inequality actually are? If we truly do not know the half of it, it is not because of any technical obstacle – only the lack of political commitment to counting.

Financial Secrecy Jurisdictions

It is rather ironical that the European based Transparency International does not think it proper to list Switzerland as the first or second most corrupt nation in the world for harbouring, encouraging and enticing all robbers of public treasuries around the world to bring their loot for safe-keeping in their dirty vaults.

Nigerian minister Professor Aliya Babs Fafunwa, on negotiating with Switzerland for the returns of assets stolen by former president Sani Abacha.[19]

The CPI identifies Africa as the most corrupt region of the world, accounting for over half of the 'most corrupt' quintile of countries in the 2006 index. A critical examination of the index, however, reveals that 53 per cent of the countries identified by the CPI as 'least corrupt' are offshore tax havens.

John Christensen[20]

Back in the 2000s, the dominant narrative was of corruption as a problem of, and for, poor countries – and especially African ones. In the context of the MDGs, this translated bluntly into *your* corruption being the reason why *our* aid is not delivering better results. The key piece of 'uncounting' behind this view was Transparency International's Corruption Perceptions Index (CPI).[21] As its website puts it today: 'Since its inception in 1995, the Corruption Perceptions Index, Transparency International's flagship research product, has become the leading global indicator of public sector corruption. The index offers an annual snapshot of the relative degree of corruption by ranking countries and territories from all over the globe.'[22]

For a perceptions-based index, the question of whose perceptions are being counted is crucial. In the case of the CPI, there may be 13 different surveys being aggregated, but there is a striking commonality in the people whose perceptions are assessed: 'a group of country economists', 'recognized country experts', 'two experts per country', 'experts based primarily in London (but also in New York, Hong Kong, Beijing and Shanghai) who are supported by a global network of in-country specialists', 'staff and consultants', 'over 100 in-house country specialists, who also draw on the expert opinions of in-country freelancers, clients and other contacts', '4,200 business executives', '100 business executives ... in each country', 'staff', '100 business executives from 30 different countries/territories', 'staff (experts)', '100 business executives per country/ territory' and, finally, 'over 2,000 experts and 66,000 other individuals from around the world have participated [to date]'.[23]

An attempt to replace perceptions with objectively verifiable evaluation came from the Tax Justice Network in the form of the Financial Secrecy Index (FSI) – a piece of counting designed to quantify a quite different narrative. The FSI rests on detailed analysis of the various aspects of financial opacity and legal, judicial and administrative cooperation, which are then combined into 20 key financial secrecy indicators under four main headings, as set out in Table 6. These cover, respectively, transparency of ownership, including of bank accounts; transparency of legal entities, including company accounts; broader assessment of the tax and financial regulatory system; and international cooperation. The resulting overall secrecy scores are then combined with measures of each jurisdiction's global importance in the provision of financial services to non-residents.[24]

The role of scale is important to ensure that the real threat is understood. For example, the US is somewhat less secretive than Nauru (a secrecy score of 60 out of 100, compared to Nauru's 67). But the US is responsible for 22.30 per cent of the total global provision of financial services to people from elsewhere. Nauru is responsible for 0.00 per cent. A pure secrecy ranking would suggest that it is Nauru that must tighten its controls, and we wouldn't argue against that. But if policymakers are interested in reducing the scale of the global threat posed by financial secrecy, starting with Nauru while ignoring the American elephant would be ridiculous.

Historically, the 'tax haven' lists of international organizations like the IMF and OECD have focused on

Table 6: Key Financial Secrecy Indicators (FSI 2018)

Ownership registration		Legal entity transparency		Integrity of tax and financial regulation		International standards and cooperation	
1	Banking secrecy	6	Public company ownership	11	Tax administration capacity	16	Public statistics
2	Trusts and foundations register	7	Public company accounts	12	Consistent personal income tax	17	Anti-money laundering
3	Recorded company ownership	8	Country by country reporting	13	Avoids promoting tax evasion	18	Automatic information exchange
4	Other wealth ownership	9	Corporate tax disclosure	14	Tax court secrecy	19	Bilateral treaties
5	Limited partnership transparency	10	Legal entity identifier	15	Harmful structures	20	International legal cooperation

the smallest jurisdictions, while being unable to confront the major players. The FSI sets out to challenge this too. The resulting ranking is intended to capture the relative threat posed by each jurisdiction, in terms of driving corruption (including tax abuses) elsewhere. It tells a very different story from the CPI. In 2018, for example, three countries featured in both the top ten 'perceived' in the CPI as least corrupt, and also in the FSI's top ten as posing the biggest global threat: Singapore, Switzerland and Luxembourg.

Table 7 provides a comparison of the top ten jurisdictions on the overall index, against the most secretive top ten and the biggest ten by scale. The differences in overall scale, and in average secrecy, are shown at the bottom of the table. The most secretive ten jurisdictions average an unweighted secrecy score of more than 80 out of 100, but are responsible in total for only around a third of 1 per cent of the global total of financial services exports. The biggest ten jurisdictions account for nearly 80 per cent of the total, and have a mean secrecy score of 61. The top

Table 7: Financial Secrecy Index 2018, top 10 by rank, secrecy and scale

Rank	Financial Secrecy Index	Secrecy Score (SS)	Global Scale Weight (GSW)
1	Switzerland	Vanuatu	USA
2	USA	Antigua and Barbuda	United Kingdom
3	Cayman Islands	Bahamas	Luxembourg
4	Hong Kong	Paraguay	Germany
5	Singapore	Brunei	Singapore
6	Luxembourg	UAE (Dubai)	Switzerland
7	Germany	Maldives	Hong Kong
8	Taiwan	Bolivia	Cayman Islands
9	UAE (Dubai)	Kenya	Ireland
10	Guernsey	Thailand	France
GSW	57.8%	0.35%	79.2%
Mean SS	69.6	83.4	60.9

Source: Financial Secrecy Index 2018, Tax Justice Network.

ten on the FSI reflect the combination of secrecy and scale, account for 58 per cent of financial services exports and have a mean secrecy score of 70. These jurisdictions, led by Switzerland and the USA, are not the most secretive but they are responsible for the most secrecy in global financial services – and therefore the greatest threat of corruption elsewhere.

A narrative that sees corruption in lower-income countries only will miss a key driver of the problem. A narrative that sees only the financial secrecy of small jurisdictions will fail to address the big players. Both mistakes, arguably, are the result of power's distorting effect on evaluation: and in different ways, both reflect the unwillingness of major economies to contemplate their own role in corruption.

A narrative that instead recognizes the centrality of financial secrecy does not ask, 'Why is your country corrupt?'. It asks, 'What are the drivers of corruption – and where?'. From the first edition of the Financial Secrecy Index in 2009, that new narrative began to become embedded. Successive 'tax haven' or 'non-cooperative jurisdiction' lists of international institutions have now introduced objectively verifiable criteria.

Two stand out. First, the 2009 G20/OECD list. This was widely derided for being largely empty before the ink was dry, and the London summit at which it appeared was also held up to ridicule for the various pronouncements made by national leaders stating that bank secrecy and the era of tax havens were over. But the list itself confirmed the important principle, even if the objectively verifiable criterion in question was to have signed a handful of agreements to exchange tax information 'upon request'.

Following in this vein, the current EU list is the clear world leader in terms of the depth and robustness of its criteria. These remain only partially objectively verifiable because key elements of the evaluation take place in private, and because the criteria are never to be applied equally to EU member states. But the breadth of the indicators, including financial secrecy and profit shifting, is the closest institutional list to the FSI; and the broad transparency is sufficient to allow an approximate application to be carried out by independent researchers.

Taking up that challenge in 2017, before the first EU list was published, Wouter Lips and I identified 60 non-EU jurisdictions that fail to meet the criteria, of which we think 41 should be listed, and an additional six EU member states: Cyprus, Ireland, Luxembourg, Malta, Netherlands and the United Kingdom.[25] The EU eventually listed 17 jurisdictions, with a further 41 committing to make changes in order to avoid listing, a group that in total mapped closely to our findings. Subsequent updates have seen both additions and removals, suggesting the process continues to be dynamic.

Power remains ever present however, with the EU unable as yet to list the US even as the latter's non-compliance with underlying OECD standards becomes ever clearer. To show that, it is useful to outline the core policy agenda in a little more detail – which also illustrates once again the risks of technical progress going ahead of full political commitment when challenging the uncounted.

The ABC of Tax Transparency

Following the formal establishment of the Tax Justice Network in 2003, internationally engaged experts from law, accounting, economics and other fields contributed to the development of a policy platform to challenge the problems of tax havenry and associated evasion and avoidance – not least by addressing the power and inequality associated with the uncounted at the top.

The core of this policy platform is the ABC of tax transparency, which responds to each of the key tools highlighted in this chapter – hidden bank accounts, hidden ownership and opaque company accounts:

- Automatic, multilateral exchange of tax information;
- Beneficial ownership (public registers for companies, trusts and foundations); and
- Country-by-country reporting by multinational companies, in public.

The A and B relate primarily to the financial secrecy sphere. Automatic exchange of tax information was intended as a direct challenge to the then OECD standard of information exchange 'upon request'. This required requesting authorities to lay out substantial details of the individual they were examining, and whose bank account information they sought. This meant not only that the requesting authorities had to know a great deal before they could ask for more, but it also in turn allowed secrecy jurisdictions multiple opportunities to stall and to reject requests on spurious grounds. In contrast, *automatic* exchange provides for regular (e.g., annual) multilateral exchange of data about all relevant accountholders – literally, the end of banking secrecy if fully delivered.

Public registers of beneficial ownership are intended to eliminate secret ownership of assets. This can occur through anonymously held vehicles including companies, trusts and foundations, or other legal structures that can play the equivalent role of separating a warm-blooded individual from that which they control and/or from which they benefit financially. As the World Bank's *Puppet Masters* research powerfully demonstrated, and as successive leaks, including the Panama Papers and Paradise Papers, have confirmed to a global public, this secrecy lies at the heart not only of much offshore tax evasion but a range of other criminal and corrupt practices. Public registers are a critical step towards ending the associated impunity.

The C of tax transparency refers to public, country-by-country reporting by multinational companies.[26] This requires data, for each jurisdiction of operation, on the absolute levels of economic activity, including sales and employment; on declared profits and tax paid; and on the names of each entity operating there, which forms part of the multinational group in question. Making this public would put multinationals on a similar transparency footing to single-country businesses, and would demonstrate the extent and nature of engineered divergence between where activity takes place and where the resulting profits are declared – a powerful tool for accountability of both multinationals themselves and of the jurisdictions that set out to procure profit shifting at the expense of their global neighbours.

While international organizations such as the OECD initially wrote off the ABC proposals as utopian and unrealistic, they quickly gained traction and by 2013 had become the basis for a global policy agenda with broad support and indeed leadership from the G20, G8 and G77 groups of countries.

The shift to automatic information exchange was confirmed with the creation of the OECD Common Reporting Standard, a fully multilateral instrument with more than 100 signatories exchanging information by September 2018 at the latest, including all the major financial centres except the United States. This represents major progress, with the structure and expectations of transparency now in place. But there is enormous work to be done in countering efforts at circumvention, and above all in ensuring full inclusion of lower-income countries. The rejectionist approach of the US, despite the standard having been initiated following its own unilateral demand for automatic information provision (through FATCA, the Foreign Account Tax Compliance Act), has opened the way for many other jurisdictions to deny information to some other signatories. For example, Switzerland will only exchange information with large trading partners, or those with a big enough stick to demand it.

On beneficial ownership, public registers are now emerging as the international standard – despite the concerted resistance of a range of small jurisdictions and individual US states that profit from selling secrecy structures. Gradually – including through the UK establishment of a public register for companies in 2016, subsequent revisions to the EU anti-money laundering directive that now requires public registers for trusts as well as companies, related measures such as new requirements in the Extractive Industry Transparency Initiative, and successive albeit small steps in the approach of the OECD Global Forum – public registers are becoming the norm.

The biggest holdout is the United States – where individual states have long competed with the leader, Delaware, for the fees associated with providing anonymous company formation services, regardless of the damage done elsewhere. This in turn has legitimized a set of smaller jurisdictions, such as Cayman, to insist that they also need not meet the emerging standard.

Finally, substantial progress has also been made in respect of country-by-country reporting. The G20 mandated the OECD in 2013 to deliver a standard, which follows the original Tax Justice Network proposals but introduces major technical flaws and one crucial difference: the data needs only to be delivered to the country tax authority headquarters, not made public. There is a range of opportunities for tax authorities to use the data, and the OECD has committed to publish partially aggregated statistics from 2020 that will reveal the jurisdiction-level pattern of profit shifting.

Once again, however, lower-income countries are largely excluded. Six years after the G20 mandate, for example, the US finally agreed a protocol to share country-by-country information with India. Smaller countries presumably need not apply ...

In each aspect of the ABC, the technical solution exists and has become part of the norm – but the political obstacles remain. Information is power, and the access of lower-income countries to the data they need from OECD countries and their multinationals and financial institutions remains very sorely limited.

It doesn't stop there. As things stand, it may be the case that the partial introduction of these technical solutions has actually worsened the global inequalities in the distribution of taxing rights. In effect, higher-income countries and the biggest economies have seen a step change in their access to offshore banking and multinational tax information. With smaller economies and lower-income countries largely excluded, the playing field has almost certainly tipped against them – even while transparency has increased overall.

There may not be a better example of the need for political context to technical solutions. The adoption of these transparency measures through international forums that are based on imbalanced relations – in which (rich country) members make rules that apply through the hardest of soft power to (lower-income) non-members – led inevitably to their enactment being partial and to the great benefit of the rule-makers only.

The acceptance of technical solutions without an accompanying agreement to cede political power provides hard evidence in support of the argument for a UN forum for future progress – because a key part of the inequality locked into these processes has been the oversight of the rich countries' club, the OECD. But it also speaks to the need to shift narratives and norms, and the SDGs provide an opportunity to tackle the uncounted here also.

5

Tax and Illicit Financial Flows in the Sustainable Development Goals

This chapter explains the related but distinct rise of tax and illicit flows, from invisible issues in the MDGs to key targets in the SDGs – and the continuing resistance.

Tax in the Sustainable Development Goals

Just as in the area of data disaggregation and horizontal inequalities explored in Part I, the SDGs reflect a new agenda in respect of the uncounted at the top. There are three important components. One relates to the central role of taxation in delivering all the goals; one to the cross-border aspects of uncounted, combined under the heading of 'illicit financial flows'; and one, discussed in chapter 6, to vertical income inequality.

It is a caricature, although not a harsh one, to call the MDGs the agenda of aid donors. Certainly, there is no mention of taxation, which is a direct reflection of the discourse at the turn of the millennium. There was little research or policy focus on tax, and even less on the development impact of financial secrecy. The importance of tax for development, though long neglected, is substantial and can be summarized in the framework of the four Rs: revenue, redistribution, re-pricing, representation.[1]

Revenue is crucial to the ability of states to provide public services, from health, education and infrastructure to effective administration and the rule of law. Redistribution is crucial to contain or eradicate both horizontal and vertical inequalities. Less obvious may be the role of taxation in re-pricing – ensuring that the true public costs and benefits of social goods (like education) and ills (such as tobacco consumption and carbon dioxide emission) are reflected in market prices.

The most important result of tax, however, is too often overlooked: political representation. Prolonged reliance on revenues from natural resources or foreign aid tends to undermine channels of responsive government, giving rise to corruption and broader failures of accountability. The act of paying tax provides an important accountability link between states and citizens, underpinning the social contract.[2] Empirical studies suggest the higher the share of tax in government spending, the stronger the process of improving governance and representation; while direct tax – taxes on income, profits and capital gains – may play a particularly influential role.[3]

But the relative dearth of attention to tax as a critical area of development policy has left the path clear for some of the most simplistic and destructive policy recommendations to become baked into what has been labelled 'the tax consensus', which for many years formed the basis of advice given around the world by the IMF and other multilateral and bilateral aid donors. John Williamson's famous identification of a broader 'Washington Consensus' included tax reform as the third of ten elements, 'about whose proper deployment Washington [or rather, its political and technocratic elites] can muster a reasonable degree of consensus'.

The Consensus is often seen unfairly as summarizing a neoliberal worldview that has been uniformly imposed on lower-income countries. Williamson intended to describe the contours of policy views as he saw them, and the tax discussion makes this especially clear:

> Increased tax revenues are the alternative to decreased public expenditures as a remedy for a fiscal deficit. Most of political Washington regards them as an inferior alternative. Much of technocratic Washington (with the exception of the right-wing think tanks) finds political Washington's aversion to tax increases irresponsible and incomprehensible. Despite this contrast in attitudes toward the merits of increasing tax revenue, there is a very wide consensus about the most desirable method of raising whatever level of tax revenue is judged to be needed. The principle is that the tax base should be broad and marginal tax rates should be moderate.[4]

The 'tax consensus' – related to, but more developed than, Williamson's sketch – was first identified in specific terms in chapters of a 2004 UNU-WIDER book (UN University, World Institute for Development Economics Research). Christopher Adam and David Bevan of Oxford University laid out the basis, and Christopher Heady, then head of tax policy and statistics at the OECD, provided a more detailed critique.[5] The key components that have become dominant are as follows:[6]

- first, to aim for *neutrality* of the tax system;
- second, to pursue redistributive goals (if any) via expenditure not taxation; and
- third, to achieve revenues of the order of 15–20% of GDP (although revenues in high-income OECD countries typically reach 30% or 40%).

Tax neutrality, that the tax system should not distort production or consumption decisions, leads in practice to lower pressure on direct taxation, to trade liberalization in the interests of efficiency, and to much greater emphasis on sales taxes to provide revenues.

The underlying ideology is that economic growth should be seen as the main aim of policy, and that taxes are an obstacle. The key assumption implicit is that an economy without taxes would deliver an efficient outcome, and so it is thought to follow that taxes should create as few distortions as possible. But of course this assumption does not hold. In the real world, removing all government intervention would deliver chaos rather than some imagined high-growth equilibrium.

The importance of tax in state-building and redistribution is entirely absent from the analysis, leaving only an Economics 101 model of the most basic microeconomic interactions. Once this extreme assumption is relaxed, it follows that (distortionary) taxation may be efficiency-enhancing, so that even a policymaker fixated on economic growth rather than sustainable human development could not support the main policy recommendations of the tax consensus in this regard.

The decision not to use tax for redistribution relies on the assumption that governments have at their disposal a full range of instruments, not least the option to make direct cash transfers to households. Non-progressive taxation can in theory be combined with this to generate the equivalent effects of a progressive tax, for example on incomes. But if governments do not have the capacity or simply the level of revenue necessary to make such transfers, then the tax consensus requires them to give up most of their power to reduce inequality, for no clear benefit in return.

The most dangerous assumption is a hidden one. The tax consensus is effectively predicated on the view that government is the basis for the solution to an optimal taxation problem, where the outcomes concern revenues, redistribution, re-pricing and the range of economic and broader human development outcomes discussed. Policymakers and their advisers need only think of the right tax tools to deliver their preferred outcomes (or those of their citizens).

In practice, however, government itself is an *outcome* of taxation. Both the extent of effective political representation and the level of corruption may be associated with the long-term reliance on tax as a source of revenue. A long history of sustained, legitimate representative government may mean that, for the medium term, the state can be treated as exogenous. But even in Western Europe, the difference in attitudes to tax and to state legitimacy is marked, according to the relative historical proximity of periods of dictatorship. For lower-income countries that may have long histories of illegitimate colonial rule, and sometimes also more recent undemocratic governance, it is unsustainable to treat the state as exogenous in an optimal tax problem.

The tax consensus is oblivious to this, and as such is simply not suited to application – in general, and to lower-income countries in particular. The blame for poor development outcomes shouldn't be laid entirely at the door of the tax consensus; but nor can it escape blame for failures in revenue collection, in redistribution and in the emergence of robust political systems through which governments can be held to account. Bad governance is directly linked to bad tax structures – and the consensus generates these in abundance.

Practical recommendations include the elimination of trade taxes (despite this being a major revenue source in lower-income countries) and the introduction and expansion of value-added tax (VAT) (even after the IMF's own research showed this to be revenue-negative for low-income countries already struggling with the lowest tax/GDP ratios).[7] Alongside this, the neglect and/or active erosion of direct taxes on income, profits and capital gains has aligned with the lobbying of multinationals and elites, adding to the pressure on governments not to pursue more effective and progressive tax policies.

Williamson identified an important element of this when describing the tax reform component of the Washington Consensus:

A particular issue that arises in the Latin American context is whether an attempt should be made to include within the tax base interest income on assets held abroad ('flight capital'). By itself a single country's law subjecting such income to taxation may not have much impact because of the problem of enforcement, but a country is not even in a position to start discussions on enforcement with haven countries until it has legislated to impose taxes on the interest from flight capital ... Achieving effective taxation of the income from flight capital is bound to take a long time, but it would be interesting to know whether any countries have embarked on the effort.[8]

It seems extraordinary to think that, in 1990, it was an open question whether lower-income countries should even think of trying to tax the offshore income of their elites. But it helps to explain why international exchange of the necessary information was still seen as such a radical proposal a decade later.

Short-term political pressures often militate against direct taxation, since indirect taxes like VAT are less salient to voters. The potential longer-term benefits of direct taxes, in terms both of lower inequality and of stronger representation, may be sacrificed to political expediency. Such a dynamic poses risks to countries with strong, long-established institutions of political representation; it also can present a major obstacle to development in countries with less well-established institutions.

This overall pressure creates a potentially vicious circle in which governments take short-term actions reflecting political calculations and external pressures, but which ultimately undermine their own legitimacy. The viciousness may be exacerbated by the growing inequality associated with promoting indirect taxes such as VAT at the expense of progressive, direct taxation. Higher inequality tends to be correlated with lower social trust, and lower trust with higher corruption/weaker governance. The tax channel implies that policies giving rise to higher inequality will also tend to weaken governance.

The 'tax citizenship' effects of any given system will not be uniform, and therefore the inequality implications of taxation go far beyond any immediate redistribution. Consider Figure 2, which shows the proportion of income paid in direct and indirect taxes by households at different income levels. The data relate to Brazil in the mid-2000s, and are extreme; but the overall pattern is not unfamiliar to countries at both lower and higher levels of per capita income.

The first panel shows the encouragingly progressive pattern of direct taxation, rising steadily from 3 per cent of the income of the lowest-income household to 10 per cent for the highest-income group. The second panel shows indirect taxes, with the expected regressive pattern: a higher share of income paid by lower-income households. But the shares of income paid in indirect tax are much higher, and so this regressive pattern completely dominates in the third panel, which shows total tax paid falling from almost half of the income of the lowest-income households, to just a quarter for the highest-income group.

What Figure 2 does not show is the political implication. A subsequent study by the Brazilian government body tasked with addressing inequality found that it was those groups that paid a higher share of their income in direct taxes – rather than in total tax – that had the strongest sense of tax citizenship: the strongest sense that the government was *their* government, accountable to *them* for spending *their* money.[9] And so the tax system represented in the figure not only exacerbates greater economic inequality (it is regressive in income terms), it also contributes to political inequality because the greater salience of direct taxation leads the lower-taxed, higher-income households to feel a greater sense of tax citizenship.

We can go further, and ask: what are likely to be the main differences in the makeup of households at lower incomes, versus those at higher incomes? We know that in general women-headed households are disproportionately likely to be towards the lower end of the

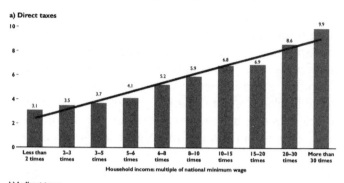

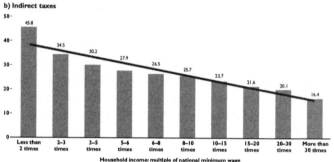

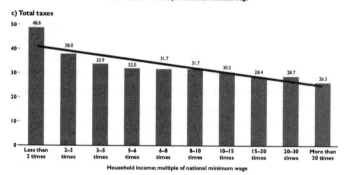

Figure 2: Direct and indirect tax and overall taxes in Brazil (%)

Source: Graphic from Jessica Espey, Alison Holder, Nuria Molina and Alex Cobham, 2014, *Born Equal: How Reducing Inequality Could Give Our Children a Better Future*. London: Save the Children, figure 12.[10]

distribution. And we also know that within households, men are (still) more likely to be the higher earners, and therefore potentially the highest payers of direct taxes (while women may be more likely to be responsible for household shopping, and so more exposed to the less salient consumption taxes).

The effect is likely to be a systematic distortion in the political engagement or empowerment of women – even when, as in this case, it runs completely counter to the relative burden of total tax. And beyond this, we can think of relatively marginalized groups, from indigenous people to people living with disabilities, and recognize that in general they too are disproportionately likely to be represented at the lower end of the distribution – and so are also likely to suffer from this added political engagement inequality.

This speculation need not imply that higher-income groups should be spared a progressive system of taxation. But it should certainly inform the thinking of policymakers about the balance of direct and indirect taxation, and about the relative burdens *and* the relative salience of tax along the distribution, if a blind application of the tax consensus would have needlessly damaging effects on political inequalities.

Paying tax is a social act, reflecting common feeling and trust in others' compliance. And on the state side, levying taxes is also a social act – providing the potential either to build the social contract, or to poison it. Tax is therefore central to the progressive realization of human rights, through its influence on the ability of the state (through available revenues), on the will of the state (through the long-term emergence and sustenance of effective and accountable political representation) and on the drivers of state action (through expressed public sentiment).

It is fair to say that the IMF and World Bank, at least in their respective Washington, DC, headquarters, have shifted substantially. The Fund's Fiscal Affairs Department, together with the newly established tax team at the Bank, are contributing to a much more vibrant set of debates and research around good policy. But worryingly, analysis of country recommendations has yet to reflect fully such a shift – suggesting that the roots of the consensus are deep indeed.[11]

A further problem stemming from the tax consensus – and also reflected in the longstanding lack of challenge to it – is the malign neglect of data in this area. An institutional failure to count, if you will. My own experience of working with IMF and World Bank data in 2005 (writing the paper that proposed the four Rs of tax) was an eye-opener in this regard. Such was the lack of interest in, or meaningful use of, the data, that it contained numerous cases of clearly implausible numbers. Most egregiously, these included a range of country-year observations where the reported total tax revenues exceeded GDP.

It took a further nine years before the launch of the ICTD/UNU-WIDER Government Revenue Dataset (GRD), which now forms a part of the international information architecture in this space.[12] One early discovery was that the tax researchers at the IMF did not themselves use their own organization's published data – not surprisingly, as there were still cases of reported tax revenues exceeding GDP – and preferred instead to rely on a privately held dataset. The initial set of papers published at the 2014 launch of the GRD demonstrated that many of the Fund papers relying on their own dataset could not be replicated, and indeed the results were in a number of cases clearly overturned by the new data.[13]

A happy effect was that the IMF made public for the first time a version of its own dataset – although, unfortunately, it continues to suffer from significant imperfections. These result in major inconsistencies in time series and across countries, and a continuing range of implausible values.[14] But at least these weaknesses are now in the open, and researchers are able to choose which tax data to use. The OECD too has since stepped up its own efforts to publish national-level tax data across different regions of the world, while regional organizations such as CEPAL in Latin America have led the way. Counting begets counting.

The neglect of tax and tax data has not been completely unwound; but things have moved a great deal since the

MDGs were established. This reflects a much broader explosion of policymaker and research interest, intertwined with the emergence of the Tax Justice Network, which was formally launched in 2003. The network pursued a twin track of building media and civil society engagement on the issues, from a very low base in each case and with considerable success.[15]

Media coverage of tax avoidance and abuses of financial secrecy is now commonplace. Stories on the low or zero tax paid by major multinationals provide a constant drumbeat for public awareness, and pressure for political progress. The role of the UK's international development NGOs has been pivotal, coinciding with a time when they were a leading force.

Tax justice did not 'become' global – it always had been. But the emergence and visibility of the Tax Justice Network allowed connections to be made with many of the national and regional groups that had long worked on the issues in their own contexts. By 2013, an umbrella body for mass mobilization NGOs was spun out: the Global Alliance for Tax Justice. The demands of the movement were heard clearly due to the combination of this mobilization, the ability to communicate well through media and, importantly, because of the common technical base on which the international demands rested.

A significant moment in terms of norm setting was the establishment of tax as the primary means of implementation for the SDGs. SDG 17 is to 'Strengthen the means of implementation and revitalize the global partnership for sustainable development', and target 17.1 is to 'Strengthen domestic resource mobilization, including through international support to developing countries, to improve domestic capacity for tax and other revenue collection'.

As I wrote on the possibility of a tax target before the SDGs were agreed: 'While the tax/GDP ratio has its flaws, it remains probably the best single measure – albeit privileging revenue over benefits of an effective tax system. The most important other benefit, of improved state–citizen relations and political representation, provides the basis to include tax/total revenue as an additional indicator.'[16] The two indicators chosen are broadly in line with this:

17.1.1 Total government revenue as a proportion of GDP, by source.
17.1.2 Proportion of domestic budget funded by domestic taxes.

While this target and indicators will not change the world alone, they represent hugely welcome progress and a clear global commitment to taxation as the means of financing development. The norm-setting power of confirming tax as the primary means of implementation is potentially substantial, and should help to ensure both the prioritization of the issue in national policy discourse and also the prioritization of lower-income country concerns in international policy settings.

Important questions remain concerning the quality of data that will be used. By and large, however, the possibilities now are far better than would have been the case had indicators been adopted in 2000; and SDG adoption will add further impetus to efforts to improve quality further.

It is also true that SDG 17.1 brings the uncounted at the top into scope, indirectly at least. The hundreds of billions of dollars in related revenue losses are now absent from global targets as well as from domestic budgets. But there are two risks here. First, that the accountability of the measures as constructed is purely national – whereas the obstacles are largely international. 'Victim-blaming' for poor performance is an obvious possibility. Second, the numbers are indirect: revenue data does not include absent revenue, and so the degree of losses is not counted here. Here, however, SDG 16.4 provides for closely related indicators – *if* the lobbying pushback is not successful.

Illicit Financial Flows in the Sustainable Development Goals

The third significant step forward in the SDGs, compared to the MDGs, was the inclusion of a target to reduce illicit financial flows. Alongside taking inequalities relatively seriously, and recognizing the central role of tax for development, the SDGs responded in target 16.4 to a final major shift that had taken place since 2000: the inverting of the corruption narrative.

The term 'illicit financial flows' was popularized by the NGO Global Financial Integrity, set up by US businessman Raymond Baker. Baker worked for decades in sub-Saharan Africa and in 2005 wrote a popular book, *Capitalism's Achilles Heel*. In Baker's assessment, there were three components: grand corruption, which accounted for just a few per cent of illicit flows; laundering of the proceeds of crime, which made up between a quarter and a third of the total; and the largest component by far, 'commercial tax evasion' through the manipulation of companies' trade prices, accounting for around two-thirds of the problem. The point of the book was to make the case that the then-standard corruption narrative missed the mark: that corruption was much less a problem of lower-income country governments than it was of private sector actors, often from high-income countries. As set out in Chapter 4, this new narrative had been growing in support since the MDGs were established, and Baker's book found a broad audience.

There is no single, agreed definition of illicit financial flows (IFF). This is, in large part, due to the breadth of the term 'illicit'. The (Oxford) dictionary definition is: 'forbidden by law, rules or custom'. The first three words alone would define 'illegal', and this highlights an important feature of any definition: illicit financial flows are not necessarily illegal. Flows forbidden by 'rules or custom' may encompass those that are socially and/or morally unacceptable, and not necessarily legally so. The phenomenon with which we are concerned is one of hidden, cross-border flows, where either the illicit origin of capital or the illicit nature of transactions undertaken is deliberately obscured.

The common feature of being hidden unites what is outright illegal, *and* what is socially forbidden – nobody wants behaviour they are proud of to go uncounted, after all. This ensures that corrupt practices that might fall within the letter of the law are included along with criminality. Significantly, that includes multinationals' tax avoidance – or, as the former head of the World Bank Jim Yong Kim labelled it: 'a form of corruption that hurts the poor'.[17]

I use a classification with four components of IFF, distinguished by motivation. The first is the abuse of markets and regulations, such as the use of offshore secrecy vehicles to build up unregulated monopoly positions. The second and more familiar component is tax abuse, including both the outright hiding of undeclared assets offshore, which is typical of individual tax evasion, and the opaque shifting of profits by multinational companies away from the places of real economic activity. The third component is the abuse of power, broadly defined, including the theft of state funds and assets, and fourth is the laundering of the proceeds of crime. The third component is close to the traditional view of corruption, and the third and fourth components map onto two of Baker's three.

The tax abuse component makes explicit an issue that is sometimes obscured in the presentation of Baker's categorization, namely that tax-motivated IFF include not only the actions of multinational companies, but also those of individuals; on the other hand, the first component, of market/regulatory abuse, is largely additional to Baker's categorization. These IFF reflect cross-border flows in which ownership is hidden, for example to circumvent sanctions or antitrust laws. Circumvention of (legal or social) limitations on political conflicts of interest, for example barriers against politicians or officials owning

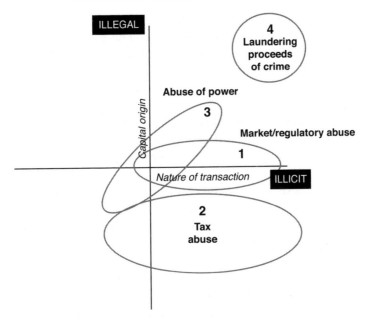

Figure 3: Main IFF types by nature of capital and transaction

Source: Alex Cobham, 2014, 'The impacts of illicit financial flows on peace and security in Africa', Tana High-Level Forum on Peace and Security in Africa Discussion Paper.[18]

stakes in regulated companies, may be included here or come under the abuse of power component.

Figure 3 maps these four IFF components according to whether or not the underlying capital is criminal in origin, and whether the transactions taking place are illicit or not. The 'old' corruption narrative was broadly comfortable addressing the illegal capital IFF in the top right quadrant, typically focusing on actors from lower-income countries rather than any enablers elsewhere. The new IFF narrative includes market and tax abuses where the capital is likely to have been legitimately obtained (typically from commerce), but the transactions are hidden – and where the key actors are in the private sector.

The impacts of IFF are many and varied, but the common element is that they are damaging to the state's *legitimacy* and *capacity* to act – which in turn undermines the achievement of human rights and development. Most simply, IFF weaken state revenues. The global estimates of the losses to each of multinational tax avoidance and individual tax evasion through undeclared offshore assets run into the hundreds of billions of dollars each year. While the losses are probably greatest in absolute terms in the richest economies, they are felt most intensely in lower-income countries, where they are estimated to account for a systematically higher proportion of current tax revenues.[19]

Since these are also the countries with lower per capita spending on crucial public services such as health and education, it is likely, in addition, that the losses translate most directly into foregone human development progress. Non-tax IFF will exacerbate these impacts also – through the diversion of economic activity into illegal markets when these generate hidden profits, and through the diversion of public assets for private gain. More broadly, markets will work less well, rent-seeking activities will proliferate at the expense of productive activities, and so economic growth is also likely to be inhibited.

The second category of IFF impact is on governance – and therefore on the likelihood of any given revenues being well spent. The damage here occurs in multiple ways. Illegal market IFF such as flows related to drug trafficking are also associated with a loss of state control, and even legitimacy, as criminal actors become more powerful. Grand corruption moves a state along the spectrum from broad-based provision of public benefits, to private capture. Tax-related IFF compound the issue. IFF militate against effective taxation, and against direct taxation in particular – thus undermining the most important of the four Rs of tax, a representative state. The evidence shows, for example, that governments more reliant on tax revenue are not only likely to spend more out of each dollar of revenue on public health, but that independently of the financing level, public health systems are also likely to achieve greater coverage.[20]

Figure 3 was republished in the report of the High Level Panel on Illicit Financial Flows out of Africa, chaired by Thabo Mbeki and under the auspices of the African Union and UN Economic Commission for Africa. That report, published in final form in 2015 and the result of three years of evidence taking, country visits and broad engagement by the panel, played a crucial role in informing the creation of a target to curtail IFF in the SDGs – and also ensured that in this area there was incontestable leadership from non-aid donor countries. Following the Mbeki panel's early work, the High Level Panel of Eminent Persons on Post-2015 had included a target in their proposal to the UN Secretary-General: '12e. Reduce illicit flows and tax evasion and increase stolen-asset recovery by $x.'

With no apparent resistance, the target was adopted directly into the final SDGs:

Goal 16: Promote peaceful and inclusive societies for sustainable development, provide access to justice for all and build effective, accountable and inclusive institutions at all levels.

Target 16.4: By 2030, significantly reduce illicit financial and arms flows, strengthen the recovery and return of stolen assets and combat all forms of organized crime.

Indicator 16.4.1: Total value of inward and outward illicit financial flows (in current United States dollars).

Indicator 16.4.2: Proportion of seized, found or surrendered arms whose illicit origin or context has been traced or established by a competent authority in line with international instruments.

The prospects for accountability on this globally agreed target now rest to a degree on the development of appropriate methodologies to estimate or measure the scale of IFF. But that work faced a threat before it could even begin. The breadth of the IFF umbrella term had supported political consensus on the SDG target. But before it could drive tangible progress, the multinational lobby had regrouped and sought retrospectively to engineer themselves out of scope.

In June 2017, the Tax Justice Network and the Global Alliance for Tax Justice (jointly), and the Independent Commission for the Reform of International Corporate Taxation (ICRICT), wrote to the UN Secretary-General António Guterres, to raise the alarm. José Antonio Ocampo, chair of ICRICT, wrote:

> We understand that some actors within the UN system are lobbying for a redefinition of the term 'illicit financial flows' in order retrospectively to exclude tax avoidance by multinational companies from the definition. Such a course of action represents a clear threat to the SDG contribution of domestic resource mobilization, and will also undermine confidence in the UN's ability to deliver honestly on what member states have previously agreed upon. We trust that your leadership will seek to stand up for lower-income countries against the lobbying of special interests in what we consider is a critical element of the global commitment towards eradicating poverty and transforming economies through sustainable development.[21]

Concerns about increased lobbying had come to a head when responsibility for the development of indicators for SDG 16.4 was handed unexpectedly to the UN Office for Drugs and Crime (UNODC) – which, as the name suggests, has no experience or expertise in working on tax or other legal capital IFF.

There are three main reasons why multinational tax avoidance should remain within scope of the IFF target. First, the definitional questions discussed above. Illicit is not synonymous with illegal, so the scope should not be limited to tax *evasion*; in additional, a significant part of avoidance is unlawful, so should not be excluded even if a strictly legal approach were to be taken. Second, in terms of impact, estimates of the scale of avoidance as discussed above are likely to be both the most robust available and to account for the largest share of IFF overall.

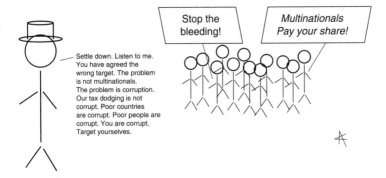

Figure 4: Lobbying to subvert the Sustainable Development Goals
Source: Tax Justice Network (https://www.taxjustice.net/2017/06/01/ subversion-sdg-16-4/).

Third, and most important, is the political legitimacy of the SDGs: this is what was globally agreed in 2015. This is worth laying out in more detail, because some have tried to claim otherwise based on the frequent sightings (and citings) of the definition used by Global Financial Integrity (GFI) – namely, illegal movements of money or capital from one country to another, 'when the funds are illegally earned, transferred, and/or utilized'. Maya Forstater, then a visiting fellow at the Center for Global Development, collected references to that phrase from reports by a number of international organizations, and argues that there was no consensus on avoidance being included in IFFs.[22]

This approach is flawed, for a couple of reasons. First, GFI was established by Raymond Baker in order to promote the concerns expressed in his 2005 book – specifically, the concerns that 'commercial tax evasion' was the biggest part of what GFI labelled illicit financial flows. The first chapter is starkly titled 'Global Capitalism: Savior or Predator?', and the emphasis is clear from the first paragraph:

'I'm not trying to make a profit!' This rocks me back on my heels. It's 1962, and I have recently taken over management of an enterprise in Nigeria. The director of the John Holt Trading Company, a British-owned firm active since the 1800s, is enlightening me about how his company does business in Africa. When I ask how he prices his imported cars, building materials and consumer goods, he adds, 'Pricing's not a problem. I'm just trying to generate high turnover.'[23]

Baker goes on to lay out powerfully how the abusive behaviour of multinationals of the period led to massive trade mispricing, and stripped lower-income host countries of their taxing rights. The same manipulation of prices for intragroup trading is the basis for most profit shifting, whether it relates to physical commodities or, increasingly these days, to intangibles like intellectual property, management services and intragroup lending. On the grounds that Baker considered this behaviour illegal, and labelled it as evasion, it seems highly unlikely that the original GFI definition was ever intended to exclude multinationals from scope – or what we politely refer to as their tax avoidance.

We also know that Baker sat on the body responsible for the most important single document underpinning the SDG target: the High Level Panel on Illicit Financial Flows from Africa. The panel report therefore adopted the GFI language, and so is cited by Forstater in support of her view that this definition was dominant *and therefore excluded multinational avoidance*. In fact, the report provides the most compelling case that avoidance was understood to be firmly in scope. The quoted GFI definition is followed by the statement: 'We also felt that the term "illicit" is a fair description of activities that, while not strictly illegal in all cases, go against established rules and norms, including avoiding legal obligations to pay tax',[24] and the document spends more time discussing avoidance than anything else:

> [W]e are convinced that success in addressing IFFs is ultimately a political issue. Issues involving abusive transfer pricing, trade misinvoicing, tax evasion, aggressive tax avoidance, double taxation, tax incentives, unfair contracts, financial secrecy, money laundering, smuggling,

trafficking and abuse of entrusted power and their interre-
lationships confer a very technical character to the study
of IFFs. However, the nature of actors, the cross-border
character of the phenomenon and the effect of IFFs on
state and society attest to the political importance of the
topic.[25]

The report of the High Level Panel of Eminent Persons
on Post-2015 is, as noted, the core document in general
for the subsequently agreed SDGs, so it is also worth
examining in a little detail. Two points are notable: first,
that the panel reflects the 'new' corruption narrative,
and second, that multinational avoidance is a repeated
theme. For example: 'Developed countries ... have special
responsibilities in ensuring that there can be no safe haven
for illicit capital and the proceeds of corruption, and that
multinational companies pay taxes fairly in the countries
in which they operate.'[26]

Some have claimed that the separation, in places, of
avoidance from illicit flows, indicates a desire to address
these separately. I think this is hairsplitting, which avoids
the clear intention of the drafters. The most relevant reference is this last one, which is from the text that justifies the
panel's proposed goal 12 – which includes the proposed
illicit flows target. There is no other target in goal 12 to
which this text can conceivably refer – and so we can
only conclude that the panel intended multinational tax
avoidance to be addressed under the illicit flows target.

> Developed countries could also pay more attention to
> exchanging information with developing countries to
> combat tax evasion. Together, they can also crack down
> on tax avoidance by multinational companies through the
> abuse of transfer pricing to artificially shift their profits
> across international borders to low-tax havens. When
> developed countries detect economic crimes involving
> developing countries, they must work together to make
> prosecuting such crimes a priority. Domestic revenues are
> the most important source for the funds needed to invest in
> sustainable development, relieve poverty and deliver public

services. Only through sufficient domestic resource mobi-lisation can countries ensure fiscal reliance and promote sustainable growth.[27]

I do not apologise for labouring the point: the lobbying seeks to rewrite a very recent history, which is available in black and white. We should count it as demonstrated that a clear, global consensus existed to ensure that multina-tional tax avoidance was central to the scope of SDG 16.4.

The lobbying will continue, though, at least until the die is cast on the indicators for SDG 16.4. The response to our raising these issues at the UN was that UNCTAD was given joint responsibility for the indicator process. UNCTAD has a track record of work on multinational companies and in its flagship World Investment Report 2015 had produced an estimate that profit shifting from lower-income countries, by way of using conduit jurisdic-tions such as Luxembourg or Mauritius to route foreign direct investment, imposed revenue losses in the region of $100 billion a year. We have cooperated closely with UNCTAD to support this work.

At the same time, however, the business lobby is step-ping up its work. Various groups have begun to appear in Geneva, seeking to make friends at the highest level of UNCTAD. The most visible has been the International Tax and Investment Center (ITIC). This group began life as a vehicle for American businesses to lobby for low tax and low regulation in former Soviet states after the fall of the Berlin Wall. But it quickly came to be dominated by tobacco companies, along with the alcohol and extractive industries, and spread its reach around the world.

A key part of ITIC's strategy has been to convince finance ministers and their officials that the Center offers technically credible, objective policy advice – rather than simply lobbying for a race to the bottom. To this end, it has long played up its relationships with the World Bank, IMF and others, claiming or suggesting partnerships where none existed. In 2016, we led a coalition of health, anti-tobacco and economic justice groups to unveil this deception.[28]

After writing to the organizations involved, we received emphatic denials of partnership from the likes of the World Bank and the African Tax Administrators Forum. Many of the claimed sponsors or participants, from the Qatar Finance Ministry to Nestlé, also disassociated themselves. ITIC was forced to withdraw a whole set of these claims, and the reporting in the *Financial Times* was damning.[29] Internal debate went on, however, and in May 2017 it was leaked that ITIC had kicked out all tobacco company executives and would no longer accept their sponsorship. The *Financial Times* covered it under the headline, 'Big Tobacco lobby group quits smoking industry'.[30]

Any incremental success by ITIC in lobbying against effective taxation of tobacco companies around the world would inevitably mean higher consumption and, therefore, higher death rates, above all in lower-income countries, which are tobacco's only remaining growth markets. But if ITIC is no longer a 'Big Tobacco lobbying group', it is still committed to fighting effective taxation. Its strategy was set out in a paper, no longer public, coauthored by the former head of Her Majesty's Revenue and Customs, David Hartnett. The paper starts by noting the context, and what it means for the multinational enterprises (MNEs) that ITIC represents:

> There is a common perception that the international corporate tax system as presently constituted reduces the tax base of lower-income countries. Many advocates also feel that the lack of information exchange on assets and income streams, and the asymmetry in tax administration capacities, affect the ability of countries classified as emerging and frontier markets to realize their fair share of taxes from MNEs. This applies particularly to companies active in 'pioneer' industries such as FMCG [fast-moving consumer goods], hotels, alcohol, telecoms, food, tobacco, banking, and energy, which are often early investors in such markets.[31]

The authors go on to argue that this is a misconception (multinationals can in fact 'perform a very useful role in helping tax administrations understand their transfer-pricing policies'). But worse, this misconception can actually result in tax authorities auditing multinationals. Happily, the authors have the solution. Which is ... to focus on something else. The authors propose seven different things for 'enhanced focus', from building leadership capacity to working on 'cooperative compliance regimes' for multinationals (speaking nicely and taking their word for things), to looking at the naughty 'shadow economy' instead of multinationals. And they offer this as a 'win-win': 'These initiatives will require much less effort and expertise than implementing, say, a new transfer pricing regime, or focusing on potential revenue losses from online sales and consumption.'[32]

Unsurprisingly, ITIC's contribution to the first open meeting in the process to determine SDG 16.4 indicators consisted of two days' worth of interventions mainly suggesting that multinationals not be included at all ...

The series of meetings has now reached the stage where various indicators are being piloted in a range of countries, including our proposals.[33] In keeping with the analysis above of IFF, and the view that most IFF other than profit shifting give rise to undeclared offshore wealth, we suggested two indicators for SDG 16.4.

The first relates to profit shifting, and it rests on the use of country-by-country reporting data – a transparency measure of genuine power, were it to be made fully public. The indicator provides a global total of the value of multinationals' profit which is declared away from the underlying economic activity. The measure is by construction fully decomposable, so that each country suffering outward profit misalignment can track the scale; and each jurisdiction procuring profit shifting from elsewhere will be fully visible and can be held accountable for reducing the damage done to others.

The second indicator uses aggregate data from the

automatic exchange of financial information to construct similar measures, at jurisdiction and global level, of the scale of undeclared assets offshore. So, for example, any disparities would be made visible between the total assets held by Finnish tax residents in any other jurisdiction, and the equivalent totals declared to the Finnish tax authorities. This would allow Finland, and every other country, to identify the jurisdictions where their residents are hiding assets – and provide a very strong incentive for greater compliance by their residents. It would also immediately identify the jurisdictions that Finland should pursue in terms of establishing automatic information exchange relationships – or imposing countermeasures against.

In this way, the two proposed indicators can meet the SDG design of providing a global dollar total for the illicit flows, but also provide the jurisdiction-level detail needed to promote accountability and progress. The area of illicit financial flows, however, remains one in which estimates – and measures – of scale are fraught with difficulty. By definition, these are quantifications of deliberately hidden phenomena. And if perfect data were readily available on a given illicit flow, making it no longer hidden, that flow would already be likely to be tending towards zero.

Overall, the SDG target provides an opportunity for unprecedented progress in the tracking and reduction of IFF. It also highlights just how uncounted are these major economic and financial phenomena – and that their lack of counting is not the result of technical difficulties, but purely of successive choices not to count. If the norm-setting power of the SDG target means anything, it should be that those political obstacles can be overcome.

That norm-setting power, however, continues to attract the uncounted lobby. A recently established group, TRACIT (Transnational Alliance to Combat Illicit Trade), describes itself as 'a private sector initiative to mitigate the economic and social damages of illicit trade'. The group focuses on illegal markets, makes no mention of tax avoidance on its website, and lists partners including the major tobacco companies that were once members of ITIC. It was recently announced that TRACIT would host a major event with UNCTAD, the custodians of the tax-related illicit flows target under SDG 16.4.

Those seeking progress do not have the luxury to relax.

6

Inequality, Understated

Summary measures such as the Gini coefficient are often presented as purely 'scientific', but in fact they explicitly embody values about a desirable distribution of income.

… without introducing [judgments about the level of inequality considered 'fair'] it is impossible to measure the degree of inequality. That no such decision has to be made with the conventional measures simply obscures the fact that they embody quite arbitrary values about the distribution of income.

Anthony Atkinson[1]

This chapter considers the measurement of income inequality, and how measurement issues combine with a careless choice of metric to leave us with a falsely positive view of the societies we live in – and how achieving the SDG target was only a partial victory.

Distribution Data: The Missing Top

Household surveys and census returns have systematically excluded groups of people who tend to be disproportionately towards the bottom of the income distribution. At the other end, there is clear evidence of non-response to surveys from the highest-income groups, so that inequality will be understated as a result. This has been addressed in recent years by the use of data from tax authorities, to fill in top incomes. The World Inequality Database was established by the greatest income inequality scholar of all, Tony Atkinson, with Thomas Piketty and colleagues, and uses tax authorities' own data, where available, to construct new series of income data, with granular data on the top 10 per cent, 1 per cent, 0.1 per cent and further where possible. While there remain many gaps to fill, the data represents a powerful step forward for our knowledge of uncounted top incomes.

The size of the adjustments to inequality is consistently large. Researchers and statisticians have tended to use the Gini coefficient to summarize inequality, and it is useful to explain briefly its derivation (see Figure 5). The value is generated from the size of the gap between a 45-degree line, representing complete equality, and a Lorenz curve showing the actual income distribution. The Gini coefficient then lies between 0, indicating complete equality in a

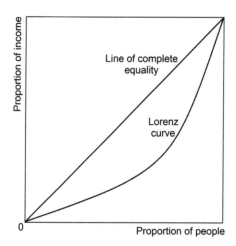

Figure 5: Gini coefficient

population, and 1, indicating complete inequality (i.e., one member of the population has the entire distribution – e.g., all the income). The figure shows a Lorenz curve, to illustrate the point graphically. Imagine that the population is lined up from left to right, with those on lowest incomes to the left. The curve then shows, at any given point, what proportion of the total income is earned by any given (lowest-income) proportion of the population.

Atkinson, Piketty and Emmanuel Saez use top income data for the United States and find that, for 2006, the adjusted Gini is 4.9 percentage points higher, at 0.519, as opposed to the original calculation of 0.470.[2] Taking a global approach, Sudhir Anand and Paul Segal, in the *Handbook of Income Distribution*, use data as available for between 18 and 23 countries for each year in their sample, and estimate a relationship between the share of the top 10 per cent and the survey mean in the national survey distribution, and that of the top 1 per cent in the income tax data.[3] Changes in the Gini coefficient range up to 4 percentage points. (An important limitation of the Gini, on which more below, is evident in the results. The equivalent change when using an alternative indicator, Theil's T, is dramatically greater at 22 percentage points.)

The second hidden area of inequality relates to income and wealth that is simply undeclared – so that it is absent from tax administrative data as much as from survey responses. Using conservatively adjusted estimates of illicit financial flows, working with colleagues from the UN Economic Commission for Africa, we found that the likely adjustments to income inequality for 30 low- and middle-income countries are roughly of the order found by Anand and Segal for tax data.[4]

Misleading Metrics: Gini vs Palma

The third dimension to hidden inequality relates to the choice of inequality measure. Atkinson's critique quoted in the epigraph at the start of this chapter highlights the particular weaknesses of the Gini coefficient as a measure of inequality. In particular, he shows that the Gini attaches more weight to transfers affecting middle-income classes. My work with Andy Sumner confirms this finding, and that the Gini becomes relatively insensitive at higher levels of inequality.[5]

Atkinson's critique is not, however, focused on the imperfection of the Gini. Indeed, he argues that no single measure can capture the full changes in a distribution. The concern is that the Gini, like any choice of single measure, will reflect a particular ideological stance – and that *this* is either hidden or forgotten, and certainly not transparent to, or understood by, the great majority of users.

Andy Sumner, Lukas Schlögl and I have argued that these hidden elements of the Gini are important for two main reasons.[6] First, because of what we call the tyranny of the Gini: that this particular measure has become almost ubiquitous in media reports on inequality, and indeed in most of the underlying research by academics and official statistical researchers. And second, because of the stylized fact uncovered in the 2000s: namely, that most of the variation in inequality occurs in the tails of the distribution. The upshot is that using the Gini is, in effect, to choose a measure of inequality that is most sensitive to changes that are less common, in a part of the distribution that we might be less concerned about, while being least sensitive to the part of the distribution where change is more likely, and which we might be more concerned about. On top of this, the measure in question is insensitive at higher inequality levels, *and* does not make any of these normative judgements explicit.

The underlying stylized fact is due to the Cambridge economist Gabriel Palma, who in 2006 and 2011 identified a consistent feature of income distributions across countries, driven by two forces: 'One is "centrifugal", and leads to an increased diversity in the shares appropriated by the top 10 and bottom 40 per cent. The other is "centripetal", and leads to a growing uniformity in the income-share appropriated by deciles 5 to 9.'[7] The 'Palma Proposition' claims, therefore, that changes in income inequality are almost exclusively due to changes in the share of the richest (D10) and poorest (D1–4), leaving unchanged the income share of the 'middle', meaning the fifth to the ninth decile group (D5–9).

On that basis, one could argue that half of the world's population (the middle and upper-middle groups) have currently acquired strong 'property rights', as Palma puts it, over half of their respective national incomes, while there may be more flexibility over the distribution of the other half of this income, between the 'rich' (the top 10 per cent of the population) and the 'poor' (the bottom 40 per cent of the population).

We used an international panel of data to look more closely at this stylized fact. We found that the relative stability of the middle of the distribution held over a wider range of countries and per capita income levels, and also across time and even, for a smaller range of countries, across different stages of the tax and transfer system. We went on to propose that the ratio of the tails – that is, the income share of the top 10 per cent versus that of the bottom 40 per cent – should be used as an alternative measure of income concentration, and named the Palma ratio.

The proposal has faced some limited criticism, mainly around two points: the stability of the Palma Proposition, and the 'blindness' of the Palma ratio to the middle of the distribution. Our 2016 paper showed that the proposition is strengthening over time. Our 2013 paper showed that, despite the differences in construction, the Gini in practice contains no more information than the Palma.

How can that be, when the Palma only uses two data points, whereas the Gini uses the whole distribution? The answer is in the regularities of the distribution of income. Regression analysis for Gini coefficients, using only the top 10 per cent and bottom 40 per cent income shares, generates a near-perfect (99–100 per cent) fit. Despite the Gini's oversensitivity to the middle, by construction, the actual Gini can be predicted almost perfectly using just the two data points that make up the Palma.

This also explains the very high correlation between the Gini and Palma. You might almost ask, then, who cares which is used? There are good reasons to care. The first is normative. A primary strength of the Palma ratio is its simplicity for use in policy debate: a Gini coefficient of 0.5 implies serious inequality but yields no intuitive statement for a non-technical audience. In contrast, the equivalent Palma of 5.0 can be directly translated into the statement that the richest 10 per cent earn five times the income of the poorest 40 per cent of a country. That simplicity makes the Palma ratio useful in policy debates, and at least as useful as the Gini in tracking inequality and income/consumption concentration.

In addition to that simplicity, the Palma ratio also helps to focus the policy debate on inequality on what can be done effectively. Consider: if the middle of the distribution already succeeds in capturing 50 per cent but they are somehow stuck at that limit, to do something significant about inequality requires moving the balance between the tails of the distribution. The Gini is not only obscure to the non-technical audience, it has also obscured this fact to the technical audience.

Lastly, in keeping with Atkinson's critique, the Palma ratio is attractive precisely because it wears its ideology on its sleeve. The focus of interest, the type of inequality that is to be addressed (or not), is transparent. The Gini, as the currently dominant measure but with an insufficiently appreciated bias, contributes to the wider problem of 'hidden' or uncounted inequality.

The second reason to care about the inequality measure is practical: sometimes the difference matters, and the choice is far from academic and can substantially change the view that emerges out of a particular situation. Figure 6 compares the Gini and Palma for UK household incomes before housing costs for 1961–2012/13, indexed to the start of the series to assist comparison. The most well-known feature of UK inequality – the major increase from the late 1970s to late 1990s – is confirmed by both measures. The subsequent divergence, however, supports quite different views.

By the Gini, inequality from the late 1990s remained more or less around the same level until 2010. This supports a view that the Labour government of Tony Blair and Gordon Brown that took power in 1997 was able only to halt the rise in inequality at most, and not reverse it. According to the Palma, however, the same period did indeed show a substantial reduction in income inequality. There is also a period in the early 1970s where Palma and Gini diverge (Gini declining, Palma steady). Whether the Gini story or the Palma is 'right' is a normative question, depending on the precise type of distributional outcome that is prioritized. What the example illustrates is how the choice of measure can reveal quite different patterns – so the tyranny of one measure can obscure a deeper understanding.

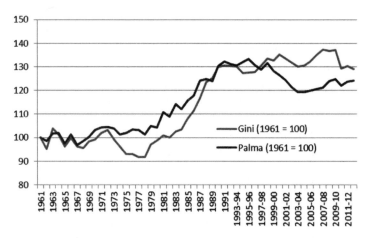

Figure 6: UK Income Inequality, 1961–2012/13 by Gini and Palma ratio

Source: Alex Cobham, Lukas Schlögl and Andy Sumner, 2016, 'Inequality and the tails: the Palma Proposition and ratio', *Global Policy* 7(1), figure 1, p. 27.

In terms of the Palma's blindness to the middle of the distribution, Sumner and I showed in our 2013 papers that the Palma ratio is quite closely correlated with the income share of the middle 50 per cent and that, in general, higher Palma ratios imply a squeezing of the share of the middle 50 per cent. In practice, the Palma will tend to reflect income concentration here too, even though it is not directly captured in the ratio.

Ultimately, the question is this. If the middle classes broadly speaking get half the national income, then inequality is about the tails of the distribution – that is, who gets the other half. Given the choice, would you prefer an inequality measure that is oversensitive to the middle and undersensitive to the tails – or the opposite?

Inequality in the SDGs

There was great concern over the inequality blindness of most of the MDGs, amplified by the growth of attention to distributional questions in development during the period (see Chapter 1 above) and also by the political tensions in high-income countries following the financial crises of 2008 onwards. The IMF had begun to generate evidence on the scale of damage done to economic growth by high inequality, bringing the debate to conservative policymaker audiences as well as to more progressive voices.[8]

The High Level Panel of Eminent Persons on Post-2015 had reported back to the UN Secretary-General that income inequality was too 'political' to have an explicit target: 'We recognised that every country is wrestling with how to address income inequality, but felt that national policy in each country, not global goalsetting, must provide the answer. History also shows that countries tend to have cycles in their income inequality as conventionally measured; and countries differ widely both in their view of what levels of income inequality are acceptable and in the strategies they adopt to reduce it.'[9] The global thematic consultation, however, revealed a broad consensus in favour of an income inequality target, and then the Open Working Group (OWG) on SDGs came down on the same side.[10]

It seemed clear that the SDGs would include an income inequality target; the question was what it would be. The value of a target would stem from the norm-setting power of the SDGs, potentially cutting across elite resistance within national political processes.

A number of specifically Palma-based targets were proposed. These included a proposal that all countries should by 2030 halve the difference between their Palma and a value of 1 (Lars Engberg-Pedersen); and that all countries should by 2030 attain a Palma of 1 (Michael Doyle and Joseph Stiglitz). I had proposed that all countries should set their own Palma target for 2030, on the basis of inclusive national discussions. In addition, 90 leading economists and development thinkers signed a letter in support of a Palma target.[11]

The World Bank promoted its 'shared prosperity' goal, which is for the positive income growth of the bottom 40 per cent of the population – regardless of what happens in the rest of the distribution. In the Bank's own words: 'We need to focus first on growing, as fast as possible, the welfare of the less well off. But we're not suggesting that countries redistribute an economic pie of a certain size, or to take from the rich and give to the poor.'[12]

In the end, those who would resist a target directly challenging inequality prevailed:

Goal 10: Reduce inequality within and among countries.
Target 10.1: By 2030, progressively achieve and sustain income growth of the bottom 40 per cent of the population at a rate higher than the national average.
Indicator 10.1.1: Growth rates of household expenditure or income per capita among the bottom 40 per cent of the population and the total population.

With no attention given to the top of the distribution, the chosen measure feels more like one of relative poverty. But there's more to it.

The target splits the difference between the World Bank's focus on the bottom 40 per cent alone, and the Palma's hard comparison with the top 10 per cent. The target is closer to the Palma insofar as there is *a* denominator (the growth of mean income), and so it is an equity target rather than an inclusion target. On the other hand, taking national growth as the denominator means that the target lacks the Palma's focus on a particular group at the top of the distribution, and supports the shared prosperity implication that top-end inequality is unimportant, and all that matters is inclusion of the bottom end.

Or – does it? If the Palma proposition were to hold perfectly – that is, if the middle shares of income were to be absolutely constant from 2016 to 2030 – then the SDG target would, mathematically, be equivalent to a target of reducing the Palma in each country.

By creating an inequality target that doesn't mention the top end, however, the SDG target allows greater room for manipulation. With a continuation of the historic stability of the middle-income share, the target can be met by a lower rate of income growth for the top 10 per cent than for the national average.

But if the elite is able to resist this, the target could also be met by a relatively unprecedented increase in the income shares of both the bottom 40 per cent and the top 10 per cent, at the expense of the middle. Is this really a reduction in inequality? This is the 'successful' scenario made possible by the eschewing of an explicit Palma target.

There are two further reasons why the SDG target is weaker than the explicit Palma targets variously proposed. First, the SDG target hides rather than clarifies the importance of top incomes for inequality. And second, the actual target (if the middle-income share was constant) is the weakest possible: not a specific reduction such as halving the distance to a Palma of 1, but *any reduction at all*.

Lastly, the indicators do not separate out the top decile. But increasingly this data is available, so tracking will still be possible – including for some countries, with the World Income Database and its tax data-adjusted distributions.

Sakiko Fukuda-Parr has studied in detail the process around SDG 10.1, and concludes that the inequality target as ultimately set was a victory for those opposed to addressing inequality and more comfortable retaining an absolute poverty focus:

> The insertion of the shared prosperity measure into the target, and into the very first draft was strategic. It had the effect of dominating the choice of targets and keeping out alternatives. And once the target was defined with this measure, it locked in the choice of indicator, and other targets and measures that focused on inequality, especially extreme inequality, were off the table.
>
> This illustrates the difficulty – or impossibility – of disentangling the technical and political considerations in defining targets and selecting indicators. Inserted into a policy forum, alternatives to the shared prosperity target were off the table because they were argued on technical merits of measurement methods. Yet for the technical body, challenging the target was off the table because it was too political.
>
> Differentiating between the political and technical is not possible in this context. Targets may be political choices but setting quantitative targets – which is preferred – necessarily requires using one among many measurement methods. The choice between the Palma ratio, Gini, and shared prosperity is not a technical matter. It is a political choice that depends on how the problem is defined. Measurement tools have different strengths and weaknesses in terms of what they measure. The best indicator is one that is most responsive to the policy concern at hand. Palma ratio is sensitive to the distance between the top and bottom of the distribution and is responsive to a concern for extreme inequality. The Gini is sensitive to movement in the middle of the distribution while shared prosperity is most policy relevant for a poverty agenda.[13]

On the technical side, the Palma has, however, made considerable strides. It has now been adopted for regular reporting in a range of international and national databases, including the OECD Income Distribution Database, the UN Human Development Report database and, for example, the household income data of the UK's Office for National Statistics. It has also been used in a growing body of academic and policy-focused research around the world. We may not have prevailed in time for the SDG target, but the possibility remains to insist on this particular piece of counting.

And we have weakened the tyranny of the Gini, at least a little. But the uncounted element of national and global income inequality will remain large, while the underlying data remains without the tax data adjustment for most countries; and without adjustment for tax evasion for any country. Unadjusted Gini coefficients are likely to understate true inequality by 5 to 8 percentage points.

The continuing use of the Gini will obscure both the degree of inequality observed, and what we can say with certainty about it. And unlike some of the issues covered in this book, which bring immediate recognition and vocal opposition, for many the question of inequality measures is a purely technical one, to be left to others to deal with. Which is, of course, just how things end up uncounted.

Part III

The Uncounted Manifesto

Inequality is what happens when we are not looking.

This is why going uncounted matters: if we don't have the numbers we can't look, monitor, track, target; and if we're not looking, the most likely outcome is a drift towards ever greater concentration. Towards greater *exclusion* of people and groups that are already marginalized, already near the bottom of distributions. Towards greater *escape* from regulation and taxation of people and companies near the top of wealth and income distributions. Towards greater inequalities of all sorts.

Consider a few of the numbers that we do have, notwithstanding the weaknesses that result from the very problems set out here. First, the uncounted at the bottom. Around 5 per cent of the world's population, 350 million or more people, are systematically excluded from surveys and census data, which are probably the best we have for understanding development and inequalities. These include, by design, homeless populations and those in institutions (hospitals and prisons), as well as highly mobile populations, including nomadic and pastoralist groups; and, as a result of sampling failures, those living in informal settlements, those from households that are fragile and/or disjointed and those living in relatively insecure areas. A similar number are from indigenous populations. Around 250 million are excluded by caste.[1] An estimated 15–20 per cent of the world's population lives with some form of disability, including those resulting from mental health issues, and the disability is considered severe for an estimated 2–4 per cent of the global population. People over 60 make up 11 per cent of the world population, which is expected to double by 2050.

All these groups are disproportionately overrepresented in multiple dimensions of poverty or disempowerment – notwithstanding the weakness of the data here too. If there were no overlap between these groups, they would make up more than 40 per cent of the world's population, marginalized and uncounted. Call it three billion people. But inequalities are intersectional, and so the total will be smaller, but the inequalities deeper. And this is without even considering gender or class!

In country after country, and in one dimension of human development after another, including the right to political expression and self-determination, the same groups are excluded – and the exclusions are largely uncounted. We all lose out from this, regardless of our own particular combinations of identities, because inequalities damage our societies in total, not just those at the bottom.[2]

At the top, where the uncounted are entirely deliberately hidden, the numbers are again necessarily estimates subject to uncertainty. But very reasonable ranges for the revenue losses from multinational tax avoidance are $100–200 billion for lower-income countries, and $200–400 billion for high-income countries; and perhaps $200 billion in total due to undeclared offshore assets. Overall, the lost revenues represent a disproportionately high share of current taxes for lower-income countries. But almost all countries are losing out to a substantial degree, with a handful of jurisdictions benefiting at the expense of all others. And revenue losses are only one part of the much wider damage, because the same financial secrecy promotes corruption and impunity that undermine the practice and institutions of political representation.

These losses directly exacerbate inequalities, through public spending programmes and through the weakening of progressive taxation more generally, and the race to the bottom that results. They also obscure our true understanding of the actual inequalities of wealth and income that exist in our societies, a problem compounded by the tyranny of the Gini coefficient as a single measure that is insensitive to extreme inequality and to inequality in the extremes of the distribution – where it matters most. Political inequalities are also widened, as the balance tips away from inclusive states and towards states that function as vehicles of private capture. What are the answers? Do we need open data? Big data? Only powerful data matters. And data with power is data that captures the whole distribution. Where our data is systematically lacking in parts of the distribution – that is, where we face the phenomenon of the uncounted – our data is lacking in power.

Data with power is not only absolute but also relative. It is data that allows the appropriate range of comparisons, data with the appropriate denominators. Where our data lacks denominators, it lacks power. We are born understanding that fairness is a relative concept. Those who control the available denominators also control the view we have of fairness. Think of the famous video of a capuchin monkey happily receiving cucumber as payment for work, until it sees its peer receive a grape for the same work, and flies into a rage. This is not envy. The object of anger is not the well-rewarded peer, but the system of ill rewards.

Or consider the Extractive Industries Transparency Initiative. Set up in the early 2000s as an inclusive, soft power approach to ensure that international companies were paying their fair share in lower-income countries, the EITI was quickly captured by those companies. The effect on the counting, and the denominators in particular, was dramatic. It was understood that companies' payments to government – in tax and royalties – were to be made public, voluntarily. But that left open a major gap, which was quickly exploited.

A denominator of the value of resources extracted would ensure accountability of the companies, by showing the ultimate share received by the countries that own the resources. Instead, the EITI went with denominators of the payments received by government (i.e., did the government declare publicly all the money that companies paid it?), and the spending made by government (i.e., did government use the companies' payments well?). These are important questions, and go to the heart of government accountability in resource-rich situations that frequently drive corruption. But the failure to ensure accountability for companies, alongside that, set back transparency in the sector by years. The existence of the EITI was used by companies to argue against an international accounting standard to address the sector's payments to government, and it was a decade before US and EU policymakers began to pass laws to circumvent company accounts and simply require the data directly. The EITI itself has now established powerful momentum to pursue real transparency, including around the beneficial ownership of companies involved in extraction – but the lost years provide an important lesson.

Data with power allows judgement of relative as well as absolute justice. We should not be blind to our cages, but equally we must not forget what we know at birth of justice, of fairness. And so we should not settle for data that lacks power. The lack of power is, ultimately, our own. It is we who go uncounted. It is our own excess inequalities that we accept if we will not challenge the uncounted.

But be clear about one thing: there is no solution that looks like a data framework. No ideal that we could just agree to collect, and thereby solve all the problems. First, the political basis for existing inequalities will not simply evaporate when the first numbers turn up. There are powerful reasons why the uncounted is a systemic issue.

Second, the issues are complex, and there are circularities in the relationships that further complicate any theory of change we might come up with.

Certain inequalities at the bottom are uncounted, either absolutely (that is, people and groups are absent from the data entirely) or relatively (the groups in question are present within the data, but not differentiated and so remain invisible). These weaknesses of the data lead variously to a lack of political power for uncounted groups, most directly when they are excluded from voting rolls, and to a lack of political salience. Groups are therefore excluded or underweighted in policy decisions, which in turn deepens the inequalities faced. Those inequalities reduce the political power of groups, making them less likely to be well counted – and so the circle continues.

At the top, meanwhile, the uncounted wealth and income of certain groups weaken the prospects for policies to ensure a level playing field, or to support redistribution. This results in higher inequalities, which in turn give rise to greater relative and absolute political power for the groups in question, which in turn helps them resist attempts at better counting – and so the circle continues.

Those circularities can work in our favour though. The naturally vicious nature of these circles does not mean that there is no prospect for progress. On the contrary, targeted interventions at key points may deliver virtuous results. Consider the case where low salience is the ultimate driver of particular inequalities – rather than, say, the Bashir regime's active preference for injustice in Sudan. A one-off intervention generating a shift in counting practices has the potential to raise the visibility of the given inequality, simultaneously improving both the weighting of the uncounted group in data used to determine policy benefits, and the group's political salience. Even in Bashir-type cases, the greater visibility of inequalities is likely to increase the political cost for a regime of sustaining deliberate injustice.

We can ask both 'What are the changes in counting that will most powerfully affect political prioritisation?', and also 'What are the political processes that will give rise to the most significant changes in counting?'. Which interventions are most likely to reverse the direction, and set off virtuous circles in which better data and better policy become mutually reinforcing instead?

In some cases, interventions will be pushing against an open door. The scales may fall from people's eyes, and we can all join hands with policymakers and embark on a new pursuit of equality and justice. But just as likely, the interventions will be among many steps needed on a slow road to making it too politically costly to continue to defend an unjust status quo. As the saying goes, politicians don't move when they see the light, but when they feel the heat. We need some hot data.

The data element of this manifesto is mainly focused on identifying some key measures that give society a chance to hold accountable those who tolerate or promote the problem of the uncounted: technical measures that are political in the truest sense; measures that really shift power. Ultimately, the breakthroughs need to be made at the relevant political level, reflecting and shifting the power balances there. But these are intended to provide the kind of scaffolding that allows conversations to begin – perhaps to inject a version of the Black Book of Sudan into the discourse, where it is most needed.

The manifesto also, necessarily, includes more directly political measures: it is the process that generates the numbers, as much as the numbers themselves, that will make sure they are hot.

We need also to recognize that any norms are also likely to be misused, as, for example, the rise of anti-terrorist norms have been used in multiple countries to shut down legitimate civil society space. Any ranking, or index or other data instrument is most likely to be taken forward when it fits existing power narratives instead of challenging them. And as in the SDGs, even apparent consensus on powerful measures can be undermined by the uncounted lobby.

Who should decide the counting to prioritize? Does it require leadership from civil society, demanding no data about us, without us? Or could a UN body take a global lead, creating a fair playing field of expectation for all to meet? And then who pays? Can the crucial role of national ownership be squared with a potential requirement for external funding? (How important was the financial support of extractive sector companies to the EITI's initial failure to count well?) And how, whether funding is national or international, can the independence of statistical offices or any other data body be guaranteed?

I propose a short set of measures. Some are immediately feasible, and even under way to an extent already; others may seem entirely unrealistic. But if the history of the Tax Justice Network teaches anything, it is to demand the impossible. Power concedes nothing without a demand, true. But demands for justice coming from millions of people can obtain concessions surprisingly quickly. What is politically impossible today can be the global policy agenda in a few short years.

The challenge of inequalities, from the local to the global, is political. Grassroots mobilization at the relevant level is the key to changing political weightings and calculations in the way that is necessary for sustained progress. But what this book identifies is that inequalities are often left unchallenged due to their lack of visibility, and due to the underlying assumption that counting is a technical sphere to be left to others – rather than a political sphere with which we should all be concerned. A pervasive failure to count leaves inequalities unknown, and removes the minimal need for politicians even to defend the injustices that result from their policies.

This manifesto therefore reflects the view that a series of one-off, 'technical' interventions can produce powerful, permanent shifts in the underlying politics, providing the potential for virtuous circles of better counting, more inclusive politics and reduced inequalities. These interventions alone will not solve the problems in each polity;

but they provide the possibility for a departure from the vicious circles of the Uncounted, onto progressive, virtuous alternatives.

These are a set of interrelated measures that can deliver a categoric shift in the transparency of the uncounted at the bottom and at the top, and the means to rein in the revealed degree of inequality. Ideally these are measures that will be delivered at the global level – but each requires full national engagement. Advocates should be clear that each step here can be taken forward by individual governments. Governments should look to move forward unilaterally and/or in regional blocs without delay, building global momentum. The necessary participation is wide, from individuals to UN institutions by way of national governments and statistics offices.

Uncounted at the Bottom

The uncounted is a debt that keeps growing. The longer people are systematically excluded from data at the bottom, the longer the inequalities they face remain invisible, and the longer the basis for policy measures to address those inequalities will remain lacking – and so the greater the cumulative denial of opportunities for human development. The data revolution behind the SDG promise to 'Leave no one behind' is not a beautiful aspiration, but an ugly necessity. It is the bare minimum, in order to stop the debt growing and to start addressing its wide-ranging effects.

A 'World We Are' commission

Consider all the groups for which we simply do not have even the most basic data on their existence, to say nothing of their enjoyment of a good life. To address the uncounted at the bottom, there is a desperate need for a baseline study: a 'Who are you?' study for the world. Such a work would require significant resources, to conduct two main exercises on an urgent basis.

One would be to draw together and to evaluate critically the kind of data only touched upon here, to understand the gap in our knowledge of major, marginalized groups in our societies. The other element would be a consultation, in the form of a follow-up to the 'World We Want' consultations that the UN conducted before the creation of the Sustainable Development Goals framework – but asking, above all, who are we? Which identities are valued, whether counted or not? Which identities are counted, whether valued or not? An international commission to examine not the world we want, but the world we are.

For each uncounted group identified at the global level, the commission would aim to establish three things:

- a baseline of the best available data on each, including the most critical gaps;
- identification of the leading partners who own both data and identities, and must participate in any future counting; and
- a costed plan to address the gaps and ensure full data on an ongoing basis.

In addition, the commission would consult on the drafting of an ethical charter for development data and that on uncounted groups in particular. This would draw out important questions of ownership and control of data and of data collation. This would include comprehensive guidelines for international organizations too, identifying few if any exceptions to when their full data on member countries and their peoples should be published.

Such a commission would require significant statistical capacity at its disposal, ideally through the UN statisticians, but would necessarily be politically rather than technically led. A key partner could be the Fight Inequality Alliance, which is perhaps uniquely well placed, as it links up national and local activism with international advocacy.

At the national level, precisely parallel processes would generate both data analysis and participative engagement on those key questions: who are you, and (how) would you like to be counted? Empowering national statistical agencies, not international or private sector bodies, to work with uncounted groups to seek independent answers could also lay the basis for stronger, independent, owned and trusted future data. Comparative analysis of national experience would also generate valuable data on the appropriate levels of funding, ways of working, relationship with state institutions, and so on.

One part of the model may be provided by the new, statutory Poverty and Inequality Commission established in Scotland.[3] The commission, of which I'm honoured to be a member, combines people with lived experience of poverty and other experts. The statutory role is to hold the Scottish government to account in relation to specific targets to reduce child poverty, and more widely on the full range of inequalities faced by people in Scotland. Drawing on the work of local groups and networks, the commission will be able to construct a meaningful baseline of the inequalities and the available data, as a basis to hold itself to account for progress also.

Local groups will include the 'fairness commissions' established in many regions and cities that use participative approaches to identify local priorities (e.g. the Dundee commission has focused on mental health, money, and the stigma associated with poverty; in England, the Sheffield commission set a target of reducing the stark inequality in life expectancy between districts of the city). National poverty and inequality commissions may provide a valuable pivot point between local and global efforts; and between participative identification of inequalities and priorities, and the statistical and policy processes that must respond. The processes involved require significant resources. Globally, there may be a role for bilateral donors in this process, but two important caveats would necessarily apply. First, a donor could not be allowed to impose any conditions other than on the transparency of the commission, and could not be represented beyond the engagement of any other country. DFID, for example, has made a welcome commitment to data disaggregation by 2030 and could on that basis provide core funding at the outset. But DFID has also pledged to use the UK aid budget only in the national interest, and so a commitment to non-interference would also be required.

Second, bilateral donors would need to fully participate, like every other country. When DFID held a Global Disability Summit in 2018, it galvanized important international commitments. But the same government has refused to fund core mortality statistics on people living with disabilities in the UK. Funding and participation would necessarily be tied. Given these constraints, it may be that foundations are better able to fund such work. Ideally, of course, governments would see the value of investing in fully nationally owned processes.

Finding out the 'World We Are' will not make inequalities disappear. But it will provide the basis to challenge: to challenge the revealed inequalities, and to challenge the inevitable drift towards being uncounted. This is a core piece of counting to provide the potential to enter virtuous circles. It should be the bare minimum that we ask ourselves, and that we know about ourselves, as the basis of humanity.

Who will count those who themselves are counting? A major risk is that states and/or elites will either actively suppress the collation or publication of data on uncomfortable inequalities, or, through inertia, simply fail to prioritize sufficiently the counting of those who are in fact most marginalized (consider, e.g., the failures globally in relation to persons with learning disabilities, and indigenous populations; or the effective absence of elites from much income distribution data). Consider, for example, the strenuous efforts of the Trump administration to exclude non-white people from the US census. Such preferences for deliberate uncounting will be seen here also.

At a minimum, reporting structures should be put in place so that the presence or absence of reporting, in relation to each inequality type relevant to each target, *is itself reported*. This would facilitate the comparison and ranking of the extent of uncounted phenomena, by issue; by inequality type and/or group; and by country and region. Is health better counted than income poverty? Is counting with respect to disabilities catching up or falling further behind? Which countries are leading, and which trailing, and why? Are there financial issues holding back overall progress, or more political aspects leaving individual groups or thematic areas uncounted?

Sometimes, such analysis will reveal legitimate prioritizations. In other cases, making the effective choices visible will ensure greater accountability, and a more participatory approach to future decisions. Underpinning this could be a version of the Open Data Inventory, which 'assesses the coverage and openness of official statistics to help identify gaps, promote open data policies, improve access, and encourage dialogue between national statistical offices and data users'.[4] If well-funded and appropriately focused, such an operation could perform a valuable role in providing a comprehensive, ongoing evaluation of national performance in measuring the uncounted at the bottom and at the top.

At the same time, systematic participation is necessary to ensure ongoing validity. The development and maintenance of questions that appropriately reflect marginalized groups and the inequalities they face is key. To this end, participation in the 'World We Are' effort should be leveraged to support the emergence of networks of engaged communities and key actors within them and without – from an Indian Institute of Dalit Studies, to a Washington Group on disability statistics, for example, to a Centro Montalvo working on the rights of Haitians in the Dominican Republic. Inequality and the uncounted are truly intersectional; participation must be too.

Participation should be equally central in the process

of gathering, testing and validating data. The term 'data witnessing' was coined by Jonathan Gray, writing about Amnesty International's *Decoders* initiative, which provided online platforms for collective participation in documenting human rights abuses of various kinds.[5] In this case, the aim would be to witness uncounting, and at the same time to collate and validate the best available data on groups and inequalities in multiple settings worldwide. An 'Uncounted' data witnessing platform could be established alongside, but independent of, the 'World We Are' commission, both to support its work and to provide external accountability of its findings.

Uncounted at the Top

The uncounted is a debt that keeps growing. The longer people and multinational companies are able to exempt themselves from data, and from tax and regulation, the greater the cumulative cost they impose – through lost revenues, damage to national and global governance, and hidden, excess inequalities. The lost taxes from hidden profit shifting run far into the trillions of dollars, ticking up by hundreds of billions each year. There can be little doubt that, since the end of formal empire, this represents the largest and most disequalizing transfer of assets globally. It is far past time to put a stop to it, and the first step is to begin monitoring the scale of the abuse.

UN Centre for Monitoring Taxing Rights

The phenomenon of the uncounted at the top undermines the ability of countries to pursue the four Rs of progressive taxation. It deprives them of revenues, frustrates redistribution, undermines the ability to re-price damaging practices such as tobacco consumption and carbon emissions, and ultimately erodes the social contract and the quality of political representation.

The research consensus is that losses to both corporate profit shifting and hidden offshore wealth are most intense for countries with lower per capita incomes. In this way, the global distribution of taxing rights is systematically skewed against lower-income countries. Worse than that, the result is a further systematic skew against the human rights – and the prospects for development – of the people in lower-income countries, and of people lower down the income distribution in all countries. The failure to count those at the top, globally and nationally, imposes needless and largely hidden inequalities.

The bare minimum to begin addressing this failure is to obtain consistent annual data. A UN Centre for Monitoring Taxing Rights should be established with this responsibility. The centre would collate and publish data on the lines of the proposed indicators for Sustainable Development Goal 16.4, discussed in Chapter 5, showing at a national and global level the divergence of multinationals' declared corporate profit from the location of their real economic activity, and the location of undeclared offshore assets: the jurisdictions that benefit from each, and those that suffer. Which countries' tax residents, for example, have the highest assets held in jurisdictions that do not provide information automatically, and which jurisdictions hold the highest assets on which they do not provide information to tax residents' home authorities? Which jurisdictions obtain the most profit unassociated with the economic activity they host, and which suffer the highest losses?

Only then, by stopping the clock on the uncounted nature of the associated tax losses, will there be a firm basis for measures to end the losses and to calculate the debts owed by financial secrecy jurisdictions and corporate tax havens. Only the United Nations can provide a legitimate, neutral forum for such a centre – and ultimately for the globally representative policy measures that must follow.

Financial transparency convention: deliver the ABC of tax transparency

Floated in negotiations on the 2018 resolution of the UN General Assembly on illicit financial flows, a convention on financial transparency would set the baseline for the minimum standards expected of jurisdictions – in order not to selfishly provoke tax abuse and corruption elsewhere. This should crystallize the recent progress on the ABC of tax transparency, ensuring that countries at all income levels enjoy the full benefits: of automatic exchange of financial information, of beneficial ownership transparency through public registers for companies, trusts and foundations, and from public country-by-country reporting by multinationals.

The convention would ensure the availability from cooperating jurisdictions of national level, aggregate measures in relation to each element to deliver the necessary data for the Centre for Monitoring Rights. In addition, the convention secretariat would be able each year to lay out data on the extent of cooperation and of financial secrecy offered by each jurisdiction in the key areas, along with the financial volumes at stake. This would complement the Centre's annual assessment of taxing rights, by identifying the key policies preventing counting and undermining a fair distribution.

Global asset registry: reveal world wealth distribution

As proposed by the Independent Commission for the Reform of International Corporate Taxation, following the work of commissioners Gabriel Zucman and Thomas Piketty, a global asset registry would connect and improve data on the ultimate beneficial ownership of wealth.[6] Potentially covering everything from financial securities to property, in addition to public registers for ownership transparency of companies, trusts and foundations, the registry would allow a comprehensive accounting of wealth inequalities at national and global levels for the first time.

The intention is not immediately to support wealth taxation, but to create knowledge and allow a meaningful discussion of societies' preferences in respect of wealth inequality. At the same time, the register would allow for wealth taxation to be effective if desired, and would provide a powerful resource for investigation and counter-measures against the whole range of illicit financial flows that anonymous ownership makes possible. The register would be divided between fully public information – such as company ownership – and information that would be publicly available with country-level aggregation but only privately accessible at the individual level (e.g., bank account information).

The overall effect would be to eliminate the greatest part of the anonymous wealth and income streams that currently dominate the global economy, driving these practices from the mainstream behaviour of corporate accounting and law firms into the backwaters of marginal, criminal activity. The empowerment of progressive taxation around the world would be powerful.

Unitary taxation: end profit shifting

The financial transparency convention would deliver fully public country-by-country reporting data, and a regular accounting of the misalignment between declared profits and the location of real economic activity – a measure that would already go some way to reversing the massive inequalities in global taxing rights that currently disfigure our world, simply by making them fully visible.

After various failed reform efforts, even the OECD is now countenancing radical reform of international tax. But this work, too, must be brought into the UN setting so that the eventual benefits are broadly shared. The replacement for the arm's length principle must take a unitary approach: assessing a multinational's global profit at the level of the group, and then apportioning it as tax base according to the proportion of real activity (employment and sales) in each country. Coupled with public country-by-country reporting, this would ensure not only that tax justice is done, but that it is consistently *seen* to be done – with clear annual accountability for both companies and jurisdictions for any misalignment.

*

We – you – need not go uncounted, nor unheard. If you share a concern for the scale of inequalities that blight our global attempts to create better societies, and to improve one another's lives, then this is a call to action. Let no one tell you the questions, or that the answers are too technical. *The uncounted* is a political issue, and the only answer is political action. Your political action. You can stand up, and you can be counted. And together we can help everyone else to do the same.

There are debts to be paid: by those who connive to go uncounted, leaving the rest of society to pick up their share; and to those who are so marginalized that they even fall out of our statistics. When we ignore the uncounted, we accept injustice and inequality. And we accept that they will go largely unseen. Let's open our eyes – and make sure everyone counts, and is counted.

Notes

Introduction

1 Michel Foucault, 1995, *Discipline and Punish: The Birth of the Prison*, New York: Random House (2nd ed.), p. 194.
2 James C. Scott, 1998, *Seeing Like a State: How Certain Schemes to Improve the Human Condition Have Failed*, London: Yale University Press, pp. 345–346.
3 Alain Desrosières, 2001, 'How "real" are statistics? Four possible attitudes', *Social Research* 68, pp. 339–355.
4 Desrosières, 'How "real" are statistics?', p. 340.
5 Wendy Espeland and Mitchell Stevens, 2008, 'A sociology of quantification', *European Journal of Sociology* XLIX (3), pp. 401–436: p. 431.
6 Theodore Porter terms as 'funny numbers', the problem that power distorts: those that are both responsible for creating statistics, and judged upon resulting metrics, face a conflict of interest that is unlikely to give rise to good data. Theodore Porter, 2012, 'Funny numbers', *Culture Unbound* 4, pp. 585–598.
7 Sakiko Fukuda-Parr and Desmond McNeill, 2019, 'Knowledge and politics in setting and measuring the SDGs: Introduction to special issue', *Global Policy* 10(S1), pp. 5–15.

8 William Seltzer and Margo Anderson, 2001, 'The dark side of numbers: The role of population data systems in human rights abuses', *Social Research* 68(2), pp. 481–513.

9 Not unrelated is the idea of resistance to the set of identification possibilities that census enumeration may require – perhaps most famously, the objection to a particular categorization by insisting on 'Jedi' as a religious identification.

10 Marco Deseriis, 2015, *Improper Names: Collective Pseudonyms from the Luddites to Anonymous*, London: Minnesota University Press, p. 4.

11 Compare Muchiri Karanja, 2010, 'Myth shattered: Kibera numbers fail to add up', *Daily Nation*, 3 September: https://www.nation.co.ke/News/Kibera%20numbers%20fail%20to%20add%20up/-/1056/1003404/-/13ga38xz/-/index.html; and Paul Currion, 2010, 'Lies, damned lies and you know the rest', *humanitarian.info*, 13 September: https://web.archive.org/web/20120803154806/http://www.humanitarian.info/2010/09/13/lies-damned-lies-and-you-know-the-rest/; with, e.g., Martin Robbins, 2012, 'The missing millions of Kibera: Africa's propaganda trail', *Guardian*, 1 August: https://www.theguardian.com/science/the-lay-scientist/2012/aug/01/africa-propaganda-kibera.

12 See, e.g., Duncan Green, 2010, 'Are women really 70% of the world's poor? How do we know?', *From Poverty to Power*, 3 February: https://oxfamblogs.org/fp2p/are-women-really-70-of-the-worlds-poor-how-do-we-know/ (and the many valuable comments); and Philip Cohen, 2013, '"Women own 1% of world property": A feminist myth that won't die', *The Atlantic*, 8 March: https://www.theatlantic.com/sexes/archive/2013/03/women-own-1-of-world-property-a-feminist-myth-that-wont-die/273840/. As an antidote reflecting the state of research beforehand, see Carmen Diana Deere and Cheryl Doss, 2008, 'The gender asset gap: What do we know and why does it matter?', *Feminist Economics* 12(1–2): https://doi.org/10.1080/13545700500508056; see also the whole special issue which it introduces.

13 James Baldwin, 1962, 'As much truth as one can bear', *New York Times*, 14 January: https://www.nytimes.com/1962/01/14/archives/as-much-truth-as-one-can-bear-to-speak-out-about-the-world-as-it-is.html.

14 On which the investigative work of Carole Cadwalladr at the *Guardian* has been invaluable.
15 Ben Goldacre, 2012, *Big Pharma*, London: Fourth Estate.
16 Cathy O'Neil, 2016, *Weapons of Math Destruction: How Big Data Increases Inequality and Threatens Democracy*, London: Allen Lane.
17 Tax Justice Network, 2015, *The Offshore League*: https://www.taxjustice.net/about/theoffshoregame/.
18 William Bruce Cameron, 1963, *Informal Sociology: A Casual Introduction to Sociological Thinking*, New York: Random House, p. 13. A quotation often, although apparently erroneously, attributed to Albert Einstein: http://quoteinvestigator.com/2010/05/26/everything-counts-einstein/.

Part I Uncounted and Excluded: The Unpeople Hidden at the Bottom

1 UN SDGs, finalized text for adoption (1 August 2015), p. 3.
2 Sébastien le Prestre Vauban, 1686, *Méthode générale et facile pour fair le dénombrement des peuples*, Paris: Imprimerie de la Veuve d'Antoine Chrestien (printed on demand, 2019, Chapitre.com). With many thanks to Dr Julia Prest for her valuable assistance with the translation.

Chapter 1: Development's Data Problem

1 Joseph Stiglitz, Amartya Sen, Jean-Paul Fitoussi, et al., 2009, *Report of the Commission on the Measurement of Economic Performance and Social Progress*, Paris: Commission on the Measurement of Economic Performance and Social Progress, p. 7.
2 This view was first sketched out, in a little more detail, in Christian Aid, 2008, *Doing Justice to Poverty*, London: Christian Aid: https://www.christianaid.org.uk/sites/default/files/2017-08/doing-justice-poverty-christian-aid-understanding-poverty-implications-december-2008.pdf.
3 A revealing story on the unsuccessful attempts to address uncounted women's work by a young researcher, Phyllis Deane, working on the early application of GDP in Malawi

and Zambia, is provided by Luke Messac, 2018, 'Outside the economy: Women's work and feminist economics in the construction and critique of national income accounting', *Journal of Imperial and Commonwealth History* 46(3), pp. 552–578.

4 UN Women, 2015, *Progress of the World's Women 2015–16*, New York: UN Women, p. 11. Statistics compiled by UN Women from various sources including ILO.

5 Angela Davis, 2018, 'Foreword', in Walter Rodney, *How Europe Underdeveloped Africa*, London: Verso Books.

6 Shanta Devarajan, 30 September 2011 keynote speech at IARIW-SSA conference on 'Measuring national income, wealth, poverty and inequality in African countries'; video available at http://blogs.worldbank.org/africacan/africa-s-st atistical-tragedy; and Morten Jerven, 2013, *Poor Numbers: How We Are Misled by African Development Statistics and What To Do About It*, Ithaca, NY: Cornell University Press.

7 Andrew Kerner, Morten Jerven and Alison Beatty, 2017, 'Does it pay to be poor? Testing for systematically underreported GNI estimates', *Review of International Organizations* 12(1), pp. 1–38.

8 Luis Martinez, 2019, 'How much should we trust the dictator's GDP growth estimates?', *SSRN Working Paper*: https://ssrn.com/abstract=3093296. Note that the result cited excludes military dictatorships, which may be considered less sensitive to domestic political pressures.

9 See box 1.1 of IMF, 2018, *World Economic Outlook* (April), Washington, DC: International Monetary Fund.

10 See, e.g., Vasilis Sarafidis, 2018, 'The tragedy of Greek statistics', *Ekathimerini*, 10 October: http://www.ekathim erini.com/233883/article/ekathimerini/comment/the-trage dy-of-greek-statistics. Georgiou recently received an international commendation for 'his competency and strength in the face of adversity, his commitment to the production of quality and trustworthiness of official statistics and his advocacy for the improvement, integrity and independence of official statistics', jointly from the International Statistical Institute, the Royal Statistical Society (UK), the American Statistical Association, the International Association for Official Statistics, the Federation of European National Statistical Societies and the Société Française de Statistique:

https://www.isi-web.org/images/2018/Press%20release%20
Commendation%20for%20Andreas%20Georgiou%20Aug
%202018.pdf.

11 James Alt, David Dreyer Lassen and Joachim Wehner, 2014,
'It isn't just about Greece: Domestic politics, transparency
and fiscal gimmickry in Europe', *British Journal of Political
Science*, 44(4), pp. 707–716.

12 Giovanni Cornia, Richard Jolly and Frances Stewart, 1987,
Adjustment with a Human Face, Oxford: Clarendon Press;
and UNDP, 1990, *Human Development Report*, New York:
United Nations Development Programme.

13 Caterina Ruggeri-Laderchi, Ruhi Saith and Frances Stewart,
2003, 'Does it matter that we do not agree on the definition of poverty? A comparison of four approaches', *Oxford
Development Studies* 31(3), pp. 243–274.

14 Most famously laid out in Amartya Sen, 1999, *Development
as Freedom,* Oxford: Oxford University Press.

15 Sakiko Fukuda-Parr, 2013, 'Global development goal setting as a policy tool for global governance: Intended and
unintended consequences', International Policy Center for
Inclusive Growth (IPC-IG) Working Paper 108, Brasilia:
UNDP, p. 4.

16 Charles Goodhart, 1975, 'Monetary relationships: A view
from Threadneedle Street', Papers in Monetary Economics,
Reserve Bank of Australia; quoted in Viral Acharya and Anjan
Thakor, 2016, 'The dark side of liquidity creation: Leverage
and systemic risk', *Journal of Financial Intermediation* 28,
doi:10.1016/j.jfi.2016.08.004.

17 APHRC/CGD, 2014, 'Delivering on the data revolution in sub-Saharan Africa', *Final Report of the Data for
African Development Working Group*, Washington, DC:
Center for Global Development; https://www.cgdev.org/
sites/default/files/CGD14-01%20complete%20for%20web
%200710.pdf.

18 Extreme income poverty numbers from World Bank data
(see Table 3); undernourishment estimate from Gisela Robles
Aguilar and Andy Sumner, 2019, 'Who are the world's poor?
A new profile of global multidimensional poverty', Center
for Global Development Working Paper 499.

19 Abi Adams and Peter Levell, 2014, 'Measuring poverty
when inflation varies across households', *Joseph Rowntree*

Foundation Report: https://www.jrf.org.uk/report/measur ing-poverty-when-inflation-varies-across-households.

20 Sanjay Reddy and Rahul Lahoti, 2016, '$1.90 a day: What does it say? The new international poverty line', *New Left Review* 97, pp. 106–127.

21 A shift first highlighted by Thomas Pogge, 2004, 'The first UN Millennium Development Goal: A cause for celebra- tion?', in Andreas Follesdal and Thomas Pogge (eds), *Real World Justice: Studies in Global Justice*, vol. 1., Dordrecht: Springer.

22 UN, 2013, 'A new global partnership: Eradicate poverty and transform economies through sustainable development', *Report of the High-Level Panel of Eminent Persons on the Post-2015 Development Agenda*, New York: United Nations, p. 7 (emphasis added): https://www.un.org/sg/sites/ www.un.org.sg/files/files/HLP_P2015_Report.pdf.

23 Frances Stewart established the Centre for Research into Inequality, Security and Ethnicity (CRISE) at Oxford, which has established the concept of horizontal inequalities in devel- opment discourse. See, e.g., Frances Stewart, 2002, 'Horizontal inequalities: A neglected dimension of development', Queen Elizabeth House Working Paper 81, Department of International Development, Oxford. The MDG Achievement Fund played a major role in supporting work that directly addressed potential applications of intersecting inequalities within the SDG framework, including the important contri- butions of Naila Kabeer – see, e.g., Naila Kabeer, 2010, *Can the MDGs Provide a Pathway to Social Justice? The Challenge of Intersecting Inequalities*, New York: UNDP, IDS/MDG Achievement Fund; and Veronica Paz Arauco, Haris Gazdar, Paula Hevia-Pacheco, Naila Kabeer, … and Chiara Mariotti, 2014, *Strengthening Social Justice to Address Intersecting Inequalities Post-2015*, London: ODI/Spanish Development Cooperation/MDG Achievement Fund. The Multidimensional Poverty Index, through the leading work of Sabina Alkire and the Oxford Poverty and Human Development Initiative (OPHI) has also highlighted the potential of survey data, albeit without stressing group inequalities.

24 Alex Cobham, Andrew Hogg and multiple Christian Aid contributors, 2010, *We're All in This Together*, London: Christian Aid.

25 Jess Espey, Alison Holder, Nuria Molina and Alex Cobham, 2012, *Born Equal: How Reducing Inequality Could Give Our Children a Better Future*, London: Save the Children; and José Manuel Roche, Lisa Wise, Dimitri Gugushvili and Luisa Hanna, 2015, *The Lottery of Birth: Giving All Children an Equal Chance to Survive*, London: Save the Children.

26 Paul Collier, 2017, *The Bottom Billion: Why the Poorest Countries are Failing and What Can Be Done About It*, Oxford: Oxford University Press; and Andy Sumner, 2010, 'Global poverty and the new bottom billion: Three-quarters of the world's poor live in middle-income countries', *IDS Working Paper* 349, Brighton: Institute of Development Studies. Collier and Sumner discuss their respective bottom billions at: https://www.ids.ac.uk/projects/the-new-bottom-billion/.

Chapter 2: The 'Data Revolution'

1 Frederick Douglass, 3 August 1857, speech given at Canandaigua, New York on the 23rd anniversary of the 'West India Emancipation': https://www.blackpast.org/afri can-american-history/1857-frederick-douglass-if-there-no-st ruggle-there-no-progress/. 'If there is no struggle there is no progress. Those who profess to favor freedom and yet depre- cate agitation are men who want crops without plowing up the ground; they want rain without thunder and lightning. They want the ocean without the awful roar of its many waters. This struggle may be a moral one, or it may be a physical one, and it may be both moral and physical, but it must be a struggle. Power concedes nothing without a demand. It never did and it never will. Find out just what any people will quietly submit to and you have found out the exact measure of injustice and wrong which will be imposed upon them, and these will continue till they are resisted with either words or blows, or with both. The limits of tyrants are prescribed by the endurance of those whom they oppress.'

2 This chapter and the next draw on my paper 'Uncounted: Power, inequalities and the post-2015 data revolution',

Development 57(3–4), pp. 320–337: http://dx.doi.org/10.10 57/dev.2015.28.

3 UNICEF/UN Women, 2013, *Addressing Inequalities: Global Thematic Consultation on the Post-2015 Development Agenda, Synthesis Report of Global Public Consultation*, New York: United Nations, p. 10: https://web.archive.org/web/20150908185219/https://www.worldwewant2015.org/node/299198.

4 UN, 2013, 'A new global partnership: Eradicate poverty and transform economies through sustainable development', *Report of the High-Level Panel of Eminent Persons on the Post-2015 Development Agenda*, New York: United Nations, p. 21; emphasis in original: https://www.un.org/sg/sites/www.un.org.sg/files/files/HLP_P2015_Report.pdf.

5 José Manuel Roche, Lisa Wise, Dimitri Gugushvili and Luisa Hanna, 2015, *The Lottery of Birth: Giving All Children an Equal Chance to Survive*, London: Save the Children.

6 UNICEF, 2015, 'Beyond averages: Learning from the MDGs', *Progress for Children* 11, New York: United Nations Children's Fund, p. iv.

7 United Nations, 2013, *Report of the UN Secretary-General on Gender Statistics*; cited at http://www.unwomen.org/en/how-we-work/flagship-programmes/making-every-woman-and-girl-count.

8 For example, Sabina Alkire and Emma Samman compare possible data sources and conclude that 'traditional in-depth survey programmes accompanied by interim surveys have the greatest potential': Alkire and Samman, 2014, 'Mobilising the household data required to progress toward the SDGs', OPHI Working Paper 72, Oxford Poverty and Human Development Initiative, Oxford, p. 34.

9 Morten Jerven, 2014, 'Benefits and costs of the data for development targets for the post-2015 development agenda', *Post-2015 Consensus Assessment*, Copenhagen: Copenhagen Consensus Center; Justin Sandefur and Gabriel Demombynes, 2014, 'Costing a data revolution', CGD Working Paper 383, Washington, DC: Center for Global Development.

10 Roy Carr-Hill, 2013, 'Missing millions and measuring development progress', *World Development* 46, pp. 30–44; and 2014, 'Measuring development progress in Africa: The

denominator problem', *Canadian Journal of Development Studies* 35(1), pp. 136–154.

11 Carr-Hill, 'Missing millions and measuring development progress'.

12 Emma Samman and Laura Rodriguez-Takeuchi, 2013, 'Old age, disability and mental health: Data issues for a post-2015 framework', *ODI Background Note*, London: Overseas Development Institute.

13 Cornell Golden, 2018, 'Summary of annual activities related to disability statistics', slides prepared for Eighteenth Meeting of the Washington Group on Disability Statistics (7–9 November 2018, Rome); http://www.washingtongroup-disa bility.com/wp-content/uploads/2019/01/WG18_Session_11 _1_Golden.pdf.

14 The ILO statistics are referenced in an interview in the UN archive of July 1989 (http://www.unmultimedia.org/tv/unia/ asset/UNA0/UNA0088/) and by the ECOSOC working group in 1991. A common reference is to the work of Shelton Davis and William Partridge, including their 1999 World Bank paper, 'Promoting the Development of Indigenous Peoples in Latin America': http://siteresources.worldbank.org/INTRA NETSOCIALDEVELOPMENT/873351-1111663716403/2 0600877/PromotingDevofIPinLAC.pdf.

15 United Nations, 12 May 2002, 'Backgrounder: First meeting of permanent forum high point of UN decade': https://web. archive.org/web/20100129055314/http://www.un.org:80/ri ghts/indigenous/backgrounder1.htm.

16 UN PFII, undated, 'Indigenous peoples, indigenous voices', *Factsheet*: https://www.un.org/esa/socdev/unpfii/documents/ 5session_factsheet1.pdf.

17 OHCHR, 2014, *Report of the Special Rapporteur on the Rights of Indigenous Peoples, Victoria Tauli Corpuz*, A/ HRC/27/52, Geneva: Office of the High Commissioner for Human Rights.

18 Resolution 47/75, paragraph 6: http://www.un.org/docum ents/ga/res/47/a47r075.htm.

19 IWGIA, 2018, *The Indigenous World 2018*, Copenhagen: International Work Group for Indigenous Affairs, p. 9: https:// www.iwgia.org/images/documents/indigenous-world/indige nous-world-2018.pdf.

20 World Medical Association, 1964 (and subsequent updates

to 2018), *Declaration of Helsinki: Ethical Principles for Medical Research Involving Human Subjects*: https://www.wma.net/policies-post/wma-declaration-of-helsinki-ethical-p rinciples-for-medical-research-involving-human-subjects/.

21 Skunk Anansie, 1996, 'Yes it's fucking political', from the album *Stoosh*.

22 Anonymous, 2004 (original Arabic version 2000), *The Black Book: Imbalance of Power and Wealth in Sudan*, Khartoum: Justice and Equality Movement, p. 31.

23 Abdullahi El-Tom, 2006, 'Darfur people: Too black for the Arab-Islamic project of Sudan', *Irish Journal of Anthropology* 9(1), pp. 12–18; see also Abdullahi El-Tom, 2003, 'The Black Book of Sudan: Imbalance of power and wealth in Sudan', *Journal of African International Affairs* 1(2), pp. 25–35.

24 Alex Cobham, 2005, 'Causes of conflict in Sudan: Testing the Black Book', *European Journal of Development Research* 17, pp. 462–480. This section draws closely on the published text.

25 Cobham, 'Causes of conflict in Sudan', p. 477.

26 As of June 2019, Sudan is governed by a 'Transitional Military Council', which has taken control after deposing Bashir in April. Widespread protests, including in Khartoum, continue to demand civilian rule.

27 Ramdane Abdoun, Jemma Dridi, Valentina Flamini and Kerstin Gerling, 2012, *Sudan: Selected Issues*, Washington, DC: International Monetary Fund.

28 World Bank, 2014, 'Sudan state-level public expenditure review: Meeting the challenges of poverty reduction and basic service delivery. Volume 2 – background papers', *Report ACS8803*, Washington, DC: World Bank. See Figures 2.3 and 2.4 for a comparison of the actual and hypothetical poverty-based allocations, of which the report notes with extreme diplomacy: 'While a formula based allo-cation appears to be underlying current transfers, it is not immediately possible to reproduce these allocations.'

29 Atta El-Hassan El-Battahani and Hassan Ali Gadkarim, 2017, 'Governance and fiscal federalism in Sudan, 1989–2015: Exploring political and intergovernmental fiscal relations in an unstable polity', *Sudan Report* 1, Bergen: Christian Michelsen Institute: https://www.cmi.no/publi

cations/file/6189-governance-and-fiscal-federalism-in-sudan.
pdf.

Chapter 3: We the People – But Only Some of Them

1 Tom Phillips, 25 August 2010, 'Brazil's census offers recognition at last to descendants of runaway slaves', *Guardian*: http://www.theguardian.com/world/2010/aug/25/brazil-2010-census-kalunga.

2 See, e.g., Margo Anderson, 2015, *The American Census: A Social History* (2nd ed.), London: Yale University Press.

3 Wilson Prichard, Paola Salardi and Paul Segal, 2014, 'Taxation, non-tax revenue and democracy: New evidence using new cross-country data', *International Centre for Tax and Development Working Paper* 23; Michael Ross, 2004, 'Does taxation lead to representation?', *British Journal of Political Science* 34, pp. 229–249.

4 Prichard et al., 'Taxation, non-tax revenue and democracy'; James Mahon, 2005, 'Liberal states and fiscal contracts: Aspects of the political economy of public finance', Paper presented at the annual meeting of the American Political Science Association.

5 G. E. Metcalfe, 1955, 'After Maclean: Some aspects of British Gold Coast policy in the mid-nineteenth century', *Transactions of the Gold Coast and Togoland Historical Society* 1(5), pp. 178–192: p. 186.

6 Metcalfe, 'After Maclean', p. 188.

7 Mara Loveman, 2007, 'Blinded like a state: The revolt against civil registration in nineteenth-century Brazil', *Comparative Studies in Society and History* 49(1), pp. 5–39: p. 8.

8 Loveman, 'Blinded like a state', p. 10.

9 Brazilian Presidency, 2003, 'Regulamenta o procedimento para identificação, reconhecimento, delimitação, demarcação e titulação das terras ocupadas por remanescentes das comunidades dos quilombos de que trata o art. 68 do Ato das Disposições Constitucionais Transitórias', *Decree* 4887, 20 November: http://www.planalto.gov.br/ccivil_03/decreto/2003/d4887.htm; and Karla Mendes, 2018, 'Slaves' descendants in Brazil braced for land titles' fight', *Reuters*

Big Story, 6 March: https://www.reuters.com/article/us-brazil-landrights-slaves/slaves-descendants-in-brazil-braced-for-land-titles-fight-idUSKCN1GI204.

10 Letycia Bond, 2018, 'Censo de 2020 deve incluir dados sobre comunidades quilombolas', *Agência Brasil*: http://agenciabrasil.ebc.com.br/geral/noticia/2018-07/censo-de-2020-deve-incluir-dados-sobre-comunidades-quilombolas.

11 Karla Mendes, 2018, '"Freedom, but no dignity" – Brazil slave descendants fight for land', *Thomson Reuters Foundation*, 11 May: http://news.trust.org/item/20180511160619-gqcmo/.

12 Marcio Dolzan, 2017, '"Não podemos abrir as portas para todo mundo', diz Bolsonaro em palestra na Hebraica', *Estadão*, 3 April: https://politica.estadao.com.br/noticias/geral,nao-podemos-abrir-as-portas-para-todo-mundo-diz-bolsonaro-em-palestra-na-hebraica,70001725522.

13 Oliveira Viana, 'O povo braziliero e sua evolução', published anonymously in the DGE report of the 1920 census, quoted in Mara Loveman, 2013, 'The race to progress: Census taking and nation making, 1870–1920', in Miguel Centeno and Agustin Ferraro (eds), *State Building in Latin America and Spain 1810s–1930s*, Cambridge: Cambridge University Press.

14 A. J. Christopher, 2003, '"To define the indefinable": Population classification and the census in South Africa', *Area* 34(4), pp. 401–408: p. 401; and Stanley R. Bailey, Fabrício M. Fialho and Mara Loveman, 2018, 'How states make race: New evidence from Brazil', *Sociological Science* 5, pp. 722–751: p. 722.

15 Rachel Gisselquist, 2019, 'Legal empowerment and group-based inequality', *Journal of Development Studies* 55(3), pp. 333–347.

16 Nicholas Biddle and Francis Markham, 2018, 'Indigenous identification change between 2011 and 2016: Evidence from the Australian census longitudinal dataset', Centre for Aboriginal Economic Policy Research Topical Issue 1, p. 1: https://openresearch-repository.anu.edu.au/bitstream/1885/148769/1/CAEPR_TopicalIssue_No1_2018%20(1).pdf.

17 Biddle and Markham, 'Indigenous identification change', p. 7.

18 Akil Khalfani and Tukufu Zuberi, 2001, 'Racial classification

and the modern census in South Africa, 1911–1996', *Race and Society* 4, pp. 161–176.

19 Union of South Africa, 1936, *Census 5th May, 1936: Preliminary Report on the Enumeration of All Races of the Population*, U.G. 50. Pretoria: Government Printers, p. viii; quoted in Khalfani and Zuberi, 'Racial classification and the modern census in South Africa', pp. 161–176.

20 A long and varied literature attests to this point, from, e.g., John Scholz and Mark Lubell, 1998, 'Trust and taxpaying: Testing the heuristic approach to collective action', *American Journal of Political Science* 42(2), pp. 398-417; to Raúl López Pérez and Aldo Ramírez Zamudio, 2019, 'Giving money to the Inca: Experiments and theory on social norms and tax compliance in Peru', *Documentos de Trabajao de Economía* 1(7) – Universidad de Lima, Facultad de Ciencias Empresariales y Económicas.

21 Gerardo Serra, 2018, '"Hail the census night": Trust and political imagination in the 1960 population census of Ghana', *Comparative Studies in Society and History* 60(3), pp. 659–687: p. 684.

22 Frederick Douglass, 1846, *Narrative of the Life of Frederick Douglass, an American Slave*, Boston: Anti-Slavery Office, p. 1.

23 Amiya Bhatia, Leonardo Ferreira, Aluísio Barros and Cesar Victora, 'Who and where are the uncounted children? Inequalities in birth certificate coverage among children under five years in 94 countries using nationally representative household surveys', *International Journal for Equity in Health* 16(148).

24 Casey Dunning, Alan Gelb and Sneha Raghavan, 2014, 'Birth registration, legal identity, and the post-2015 agenda', *CGD Policy Paper* 46, Washington DC: Center for Global Development, p. 3.

25 Bhatia, Ferreira, Barros and Victora, 'Who and where are the uncounted children?'.

26 UNICEF, 2013, *Every Child's Birth Right: Inequities and Trends in Birth Registration*, New York: United Nations Children's Fund.

27 Wendy Hunter, 2019, 'Identity documents, welfare enhancement, and group empowerment in the global South', *Journal of Development Studies* 55(3), pp. 366–383.

28 Hunter, 'Identity documents', p. 367.
29 Tendayi Bloom, 2015, '"Transforming our world" – How can we make sure no one is left behind?', European Network on Statelessness: http://www.statelessness.eu/blog/transform ing-our-world%E2%80%99-how-can-we-make-sure-no-on e-left-behind.
30 The Counted: https://www.theguardian.com/us-news/series/ counted-us-police-killings.
31 Jon Swaine and Ciara McCarthy, 2016, 'Killings by US police logged at twice the previous rate under new federal program', *Guardian*, 15 December: https://www.theguard ian.com/us-news/2016/dec/15/us-police-killings-departm ent-of-justice-program.
32 https://www.bjs.gov/index.cfm?ty=pbseandsid=74.
33 TBIJ, 2018, 'Dying homeless: Counting the deaths of home less people across the UK': https://www.thebureauinvestiga tes.com/stories/2018-04-23/dying-homeless.
34 Karin Goodwin, 2018, 'Review promised on Scottish homeless death statistics', *The Ferret*: https://theferret.scot/ review-scottish-homeless-death-statistics/.
35 Reem Abu-Hayyeh and Frances Webber, 2015, 'Unwanted, unnoticed: An audit of 160 asylum and immigration-related deaths in Europe', *Institute of Race Relations Briefing Paper* 10, p. 5.
36 https://www.theguardian.com/world/series/the-list.
37 GBD 2015 Maternal Mortality Collaborators, 2016, 'Global, regional, and national levels of maternal mortality, 1990–2015: A systematic analysis for the Global Burden of Disease Study 2015', *The Lancet* 388, pp. 1775–1812.
38 CDC, *Pregnancy Mortality Surveillance System*: https:// www.cdc.gov/reproductivehealth/maternalinfanthealth/preg nancy-mortality-surveillance-system.htm.
39 Kari Sonde, 2018, 'Puerto Rico finally admits it wildly underestimated Hurricane Maria death toll', *Mother Jones*, 9 August: https://www.motherjones.com/politics/2018/08/ puerto-rico-admits-hurricane-maria-death-toll-1427/.
40 Government of Puerto Rico, 2018, *Transformation and Innovation in the Wake of Devastation: An Economic and Disaster Recovery Plan for Puerto Rico*, Puerto Rico: http:// www.p3.pr.gov/assets/pr-draft-recovery-plan-for-comment- july-9-2018.pdf.

41 Samuel Oakford, 2018, 'Deaths before data: How war, politics, and a lack of reliable information are complicating a famine declaration in Yemen', *The New Humanitarian*, 12 November: https://www.thenewhumanitarian.org/analysis/2018/11/12/Yemen-war-conflict-deaths-data-famine.

42 WHO, undated, 'Maternal and perinatal death reviews in the UK', https://www.who.int/maternal_child_adolescent/ep idemiology/maternal-death-surveillance/case-studies/united-kingdom/en/ (accessed 5 March 2019).

43 W. D. Ngan Kee, 2005, 'Confidential enquiries into maternal deaths: 50 years of closing the loop', *British Journal of Anaesthesia* 94(4), pp. 413–416.

44 LeDeR, 2018, *The Learning Disabilities Mortality Review Annual Report 2017*, Bristol: University of Bristol Norah Fry Centre for Disability Studies.

45 ONS, 2017, *Health State Life Expectancies, UK: 2014 to 2016*, Newport: Office for National Statistics: https://www.ons.gov.uk/peoplepopulationandcommunity/healthandsoci alcare/healthandlifeexpectancies/bulletins/healthstatelifeexp ectanciesuk/2014to2016.

46 Pauline Heslop, Peter Blair, Peter Fleming, Matt Hoghton, Anna Marriott and Lesley Russ, 2013, *Final Report of Confidential Inquiry into Premature Deaths of People with Learning Disabilities (CIPOLD)*, Bristol: University of Bristol Norah Fry Centre for Disability Studies: http://www.bris.ac.uk/media-library/sites/cipold/migrated/documents/fu llfinalreport.pdf.

47 Simon Duffy, 2015, *A Fair Society? How the Cuts Target Disabled People*, Sheffield: Centre for Welfare Reform/Campaign for a Fair Society: https://www.centreforwelfare reform.org/uploads/attachment/354/a-fair-society.pdf.

48 Randeep Ramesh, 2013, 'No review board into early deaths of patients with learning disabilities', *Guardian*, 12 July.

49 UN CESCR, 2016, 'Concluding observations on the sixth periodic report of the United Kingdom of Great Britain and Northern Ireland', E/C.12/GBR/CO/6, New York: UN Committee on Economic, Social and Cultural Rights.

50 Chaka Bachmann and Becca Gooch, 2018, *LGBT in Britain: Health Report*, London: Stonewall: https://www.stonewall.org.uk/sites/default/files/lgbt_in_britain_health.pdf.

51 For the full story, see justiceforlb.org and read Sara Ryan,

2017, *Justice for Laughing Boy Connor Sparrowhawk – A Death by Indifference*, London: Jessica Kingsley Publishers.

52 See, e.g., Wendy R. Weiser and Lawrence Norden, 2011, *Voting Law Changes in 2012*, New York: Brennan Center for Justice: http://www.brennancenter.org/publication/voting-law-changes-2012; and s.e. smith, 2016, 'Voting is already hard for people with disabilities. Voter ID laws make it even harder', *Vox*, 1 April: https://www.vox.com/2016/4/1/11346714/voter-id-laws-disabilities.

53 Adalah, 2019, 'Disenfranchised: Thousands of Bedouin citizens prevented from voting in upcoming Israeli election': https://www.adalah.org/en/content/view/9681.

54 Roxana Hegeman, 2018, 'Iconic Dodge City moves its only polling place outside town', *AP News*: https://www.apnews.com/70e4a2665b0644bf884c60c25405c076.

55 Carol Anderson, 2018, 'Georgia doesn't need another voter suppressor running its elections', *Guardian*: https://www.theguardian.com/commentisfree/2018/dec/03/georgia-election-vote-voter-suppression-secretary-of-state-brad-raffensperger.

56 Pema Levy, 2018, 'After Heidi Heitkamp won a Senate seat, North Dakota Republicans made it harder for Native Americans to vote', *Mother Jones*, 19 October: https://www.motherjones.com/politics/2018/10/heidi-heitkamp-native-americans-vote-north-dakota/.

57 Mark Stern, 2018, 'Supreme Court, in 5–4 Decision, allows states to purge voters for their failure to vote', *Slate*, 11 June: https://slate.com/news-and-politics/2018/06/supreme-court-greenlights-ohio-voter-purges-in-husted-v-randolph.html.

58 Ari Berman, 2018, 'The United States is becoming a two-tiered country with separate and unequal voting laws', *Mother Jones*, 19 November: https://www.motherjones.com/politics/2018/11/the-united-states-is-becoming-a-two-tiered-country-with-separate-and-unequal-voting-laws-1/.

59 Ari Berman, 2019, 'In census case, Supreme Court suddenly cares a lot about Voting Rights Act', *Mother Jones*, 23 April: https://www.motherjones.com/politics/2019/04/in-census-case-supreme-court-suddenly-cares-a-lot-about-voting-rights-act/.

60 Census Bureau, 2012, 'Census Bureau releases estimates of overcount and undercount in the 2010 Census', *CB*

12-95, 22 May: https://www.census.gov/newsroom/releases/archives/2010_census/cb12-95.html.

61 http://prospect.org/article/insidious-way-underrepresent-minorities.

62 Mikelyn Meyers, 2017, 'Respondent confidentiality concerns and possible effects on response rates and data quality for the 2020 census', presentation made to National Advisory Committee on Racial, Ethnic and Other Populations Fall Meeting, 2 November: https://assets.documentcloud.org/documents/4424705/Census-Confidentiality-Presentation.pdf.

63 John Abowd, 19 January 2018, 'Technical review of the Department of Justice request to add citizenship question to the 2020 Census', *Memorandum for Wilbur L. Ross, Jr, Secretary of Commerce*, made available as part of the complete administrative record upon which the Secretary of Commerce based his decision to reinstate a question concerning citizenship in the 2020 Decennial Census: http://www.osec.doc.gov/opog/FOIA/Documents/AR%20-%20FINAL%20FILED%20-%20ALL%20DOCS%20%5bCERTIFICATION-INDEX-DOCUMENTS%5d%206.8.18.pdf#page=1289.

64 Arturo Vargas, 2018, 'Democracy at risk: The state of the 2020 Census and Latinos', *NALEO Educational Fund Webinar*: https://d3n8a8pro7vhmx.cloudfront.net/naleo/pages/1423/attachments/original/1524600253/NEF_Census_Press_Club_Briefing_corrdft_04-18_-_FINAL.pdf (accessed 28 April 2019).

Part II Uncounted and Illicit:
The Unmoney Hiding at the Top

1 Brooke Harrington, 2016, 'How to hide it: inside the secret world of wealth managers', *Guardian*, 21 September: https://www.theguardian.com/business/2016/sep/21/how-to-hide-it-inside-secret-world-of-wealth-managers. STEP is the Society of Trust and Estate Practitioners, self-described as 'the global professional association for practitioners who specialise in family inheritance and succession planning'. I'm grateful to STEP for confirming that the specific text comes

from the 'Trust Creation Law and Practice' manual of the STEP Diploma in International Trust Management.

2 Lucky Luciano (1897–1962) was an Italian-born mobster, who lived and operated in the US.

3 Lukas Linsi and Daniel Mügge, 2019, 'Globalization and the growing defects of international economic statistics', *Review of International Political Economy*: https://doi.org/10.1080/09692290.2018.1560353.

Chapter 4: Uncounted at the Top

1 George Turner and Alex Cobham, 2015, 'Doing SFA for fair play?', *The Offshore Game Report for Tax Justice Network*: https://www.taxjustice.net/wp-content/uploads/2015/10/Web-edition-Doing-SFA-for-Fair-Play-Main-report-update d.pdf.

2 United States Department of Justice Office of Special Counsel, 2018, 'Superseding criminal information: United States of America vs Richard W. Gates III', case 1:17-cr-00201-ABJ, document 195: https://www.lawfareblog.com/docume nts-gates-superseding-criminal-information-statement-offen se-plea-agreement.

3 James Stewart, 2008, 'Shadow regulation and the shadow banking system', *Tax Justice Focus* 4(2): http://www.tax justice.net/cms/upload/pdf/TJF_4-2_AABA_-_Research.pdf; see also Alex Cobham, Rachel Baird and Andrew Hogg, 2008, 'The morning after the night before: The impact of the financial crisis on the developing world', *Christian Aid Report*: https://www.christianaid.org.uk/sites/default/files/2017-08/morning-after-night-before-november-2008_0.pdf.

4 Simon Bowers, 2017, 'Leaked documents expose secret tale of Apple's offshore island hop', *International Consortium of Investigative Journalists*, 6 November: https://www.icij.org/investigations/paradise-papers/apples-secret-offshore-island-hop-revealed-by-paradise-papers-leak-icij/.

5 #sorrynotsorry.

6 Utsa Patnaik, 2017, 'Revisiting the "Drain", or transfers from India to Britain', in Shubhra Chakrabarti and Utsa Patnaik (eds.), *Agrarian and Other Histories: Essays for Binay Bhushan Chaudhuri*, New Delhi: Tulika Books. As cited in

Ajai Sreevatsan, 2018, 'British Raj siphoned out $45 trillion from India: Utsa Patnaik', *LiveMint*: https://www.livemint.com/Companies/HNZA71LNVNNVXQ1eaIKu6M/British-Raj-siphoned-out-45-trillion-from-India-Utsa-Patna.html; and Jason Hickel, 2018, 'How Britain stole $45 trillion from India: And lied about it', *Al-Jazeera*: https://www.aljazeera.com/indepth/opinion/britain-stole-45-trillion-india-181206124830851.html.

7 Alex Cobham, Petr Janský and Markus Meinzer, 2018, 'A half-century of resistance to corporate disclosure', *Transnational Corporations* 25(3), pp. 1–26: https://unctad.org/en/PublicationChapters/diaeia2018d5a2_en.pdf.

8 Alex Cobham and Petr Janský, 2017, 'Measuring misalignment: The location of US multinationals' economic activity versus the location of their profits', *Development Policy Review*, pp. 1–38: https://doi.org/10.1111/dpr.12315.

9 Chris Jones, Yama Temouri and Alex Cobham, 2017, 'Tax haven networks and the role of the Big 4 accountancy firms', *Journal of World Business* 53(2): https://doi.org/10.1016/j.jwb.2017.10.004.

10 Thomas Tørsløv, Ludwig Wier and Gabriel Zucman, 2018, 'The missing profits of nations', *National Bureau of Economic Research* (24071): https://doi.org/10.3386/w24701; UNCTAD, 2015, *World Investment Report 2015 – Reforming International Investment Governance*, Geneva: United Nations; OECD, 2015, *Measuring and Monitoring BEPS, Action 11 – 2015 Final Report*, Paris: Organisation for Economic Co-operation and Development: http://www.oecd-ilibrary.org/content/book/9789264241343-en; Ernesto Crivelli, Ruud de Mooij and Michael Keen, 2016, 'Base erosion, profit shifting and developing countries', *FinanzArchiv: Public Finance Analysis* 72(3), pp. 268–301: https://doi.org/10.1628/001522116X14646834385460; Alex Cobham and Petr Janský, 2017, 'Global distribution of revenue loss from corporate tax avoidance: Re-estimation and country results', *Journal of International Development* 30(2), pp. 206–232: https://doi.org/10.1002/jid.3348.

11 See the Tax Justice Network's *Corporate Tax Haven Index 2019* for detailed analysis and ranking.

12 Tørsløv, Wier and Zucman, 2018, 'The missing profits of nations'.

13 Jannick Damgaard, Thomas Elkjaer and Niels Johannesen, 2018, 'Piercing the veil', *Finance and Development* 55(2): https://www.imf.org/external/pubs/ft/fandd/2018/06/inside-the-world-of-global-tax-havens-and-offshore-banking/damg aard.htm.

14 Simon Bowers, 2017, 'Leaked documents expose secret tale of Apple's offshore island hop', *International Consortium of Investigative Journalists*: https://www.icij.org/investiga tions/paradise-papers/apples-secret-offshore-island-hop-reve aled-by-paradise-papers-leak-icij/.

15 Heike Joebges, 2017, 'Crisis recovery in a country with a high presence of foreign owned companies: The case of Ireland', *Hans-Böckler-Stiftung working paper* 175: https://www.socialeurope.eu/wp-content/uploads/2017/01/p_imk_wp_175_2017.pdf.

16 James Henry, 2012, *The Price of Offshore, Revisited*, London: Tax Justice Network: https://www.taxjustice.net/2014/01/17/price-offshore-revisited/;   Gabriel   Zucman, 2013, 'The missing wealth of nations: Are Europe and the US net debtors or net creditors?', *Quarterly Journal of Economics* 128(3): pp. 1321–1364.

17 Nick Shaxson, John Christensen and Nick Mathiason, 2012, *Inequality: You Don't Know the Half of It (Or Why Inequality Is Worse Than We Thought)*, London: Tax Justice Network: https://www.taxjustice.net/wp-content/uploads/2013/04/Inequality-1207-you-dont-know-the-half-of-it.pdf.

18 Gabriel Zucman, 2019, 'Global wealth inequality', NBER working paper 25462; Annette Alstadsæter, Niels Johannesen and Gabriel Zucman, 2018, 'Who owns the wealth in tax havens? Macro evidence and implications for global inequality', *Journal of Public Economics* 162, pp. 89–100.

19 Quoted in *This Day*, 6 June 2005, by John Christensen, 2007, 'Mirror, mirror, on the wall, who's the most corrupt of all?', *Tax Justice Network*: https://taxjustice.net/cms/up load/pdf/0701_Mirror_Mirror_corruption.pdf.

20 Christensen, 'Mirror, mirror, on the wall', p. 3.

21 An important moment in the gradual inversion of this narrative was John Christensen's seminal paper, 'Mirror, mirror, on the wall', delivered at the World Social Forum in Nairobi in January 2007, where the Tax Justice Network – Africa was also launched. As well as highlighting the CPI's favourable

treatment of tax havens as above, Christensen wrote: 'It is debatable whether TI [Transparency International] intended to shape the corruption debate in this way, but the tendency to treat corruption as synonymous with bribery of public sector officials is partly due to the methodology of the CPI, which draws on the perceptions of businesses and a narrow range of think tanks. Unsurprisingly this community has tended to concentrate on those areas of corruption which impose a cost on business, bribery and kickbacks being the foremost issue of concern in this respect, without paying attention to issues such as tax evasion and trade mispricing which involve business imposing costs on the rest of society. Concerns have been expressed about the methodological biases of the CPI, and critics argue that the index distorts the geography of corruption by reinforcing negative images of developing countries and ignoring the higher level corruption of major companies and governments from the North' ('Mirror, mirror, on the wall', p. 3). Christensen's paper was an important catalyst for the tax justice discussions that took part in Nairobi and culminated in a decision to create the Financial Secrecy Index.

22 https://www.transparency.org/cpi2018.
23 See Alex Cobham, 2013, 'Corrupting perceptions: Why Transparency International's flagship corruption index falls short', *Foreign Policy*, 22 July: https://foreignpolicy.com/2013/07/22/corrupting-perceptions/.
24 For full details on the technical basis for the index construction, see Alex Cobham, Petr Janský and Markus Meinzer, 2015, 'The Financial Secrecy Index: Shedding new light on the geography of secrecy', *Economic Geography* 91(3), pp. 281–303. The latest methodology, results, data and visualizations are available at http://financialsecrecyindex.com.
25 Wouter Lips and Alex Cobham, 2017, 'Paradise lost: Who will feature on the common EU blacklist of non-cooperative tax jurisdictions?', *Open Data for Tax Justice*: http://datafortaxjustice.net/paradiselost. Cf. http://europa.eu/rapid/press-release_IP-17-5121_en.htm.
26 While the idea has roots in UN debates going back to the 1960s at least, the first draft international accounting standard for country-by-country reporting was proposed in 2003, by Richard Murphy for the Association of Accounting and

Business Affairs and the Tax Justice Network. See Alex Cobham, Jonathan Gray and Richard Murphy, 2017, 'What do they pay?' CITYPERC Working Paper 2017/01, London: http://www.city.ac.uk/__data/assets/pdf_file/0004/345469/C ITYPERC-WPS-201701.pdf.

Chapter 5: Tax and Illicit Financial Flows in the Sustainable Development Goals

1 Alex Cobham, 2005, 'Taxation policy and development', *OCGG Economy Analysis* 2, Oxford: Oxford Council on Good Governance; http://taxjustice.net/cms/upload/pdf/OC GG_-_Alex_Cobham_-_Taxation_Policy_and_Development .pdf.

2 Deborah Brautigam, Odd-Helge Fjeldstad and Mick Moore (eds.), 2008, *Taxation and State Building in Developing Countries*, Cambridge: Cambridge University Press; Rasmus Broms, 2011, 'Taxation and government quality: The size, the shape, or just Europe 300 years ago?', Quality of Government Institute (University of Gothenburg) Working Paper 16.

3 Michael Ross, 2004, 'Does taxation lead to representation?', *British Journal of Political Science* 34, pp. 229–249; and powerfully confirmed with much stronger data by Wilson Prichard, Paola Salardi and Paul Segal, 2014, 'Taxation, non-tax revenue and democracy: New evidence using new cross-country data', International Centre for Tax and Development Working Paper 23. On the role of direct tax, see also James Mahon, 2005, 'Liberal states and fiscal contracts: Aspects of the political economy of public finance', Paper presented at the annual meeting of the American Political Science Association.

4 John Williamson, 1990, 'What Washington means by policy reform', in Williamson (ed.), *Latin American Adjustment: How Much Has Happened?*, Washington, DC: Institute for International Economics, ch. 2: https://piie.com/comment ary/speeches-papers/what-washington-means-policy-reform.

5 Christopher Adam and David Bevan, 2004, 'Fiscal policy design in low-income countries', and Christopher Heady, 2004, 'Taxation policy in low-income countries', in Tony

Addison and Alan Roe (eds), *Fiscal Policy for Development*, Basingstoke: Palgrave Macmillan/UNU-WIDER.

6 This discussion draws on my paper, 'The tax consensus has failed!', Oxford Council on Good Governance Economy Section Recommendation 8: http://taxjustice.net/cms/upload/pdf/Cobham_Tax_Consensus_Failed_08.pdf.

7 Thomas Baunsgaard and Michael Keen, 2005, 'Tax revenue and (or?) trade liberalization', IMF Working Paper WP/05/112.

8 Williamson, 'What Washington means by policy reform'.

9 CDES (Economic and Social Development Council of Brazil), 2011, 'Inequity indicators of the national tax system', *Observation Report* 2.

10 https://www.savethechildren.org.uk/content/dam/global/reports/advocacy/born-equal.pdf. Original sourcing: CDES, 'Inequity indicators of the national tax system'; and M. H. Zockun, H. Zylberstajn, S. Silber, J. Rizzieri, A. Portela, E. Pellin and L. E. Afonso, 2007, 'Simplificando O Brasil: Propostas de reforma na relação econômica do governo com o setor privado', *Fundação Instituto De Pesquisas Econômicas (FIPE) Texto Para Discussão* 03, Table 6. The columns show the tax burden on groups in Brazil, according to whether household income is less than two times the national minimum wage, 2–3 times the minimum wage, and so on, up to incomes exceeding 30 times the minimum wage: http://www.fipe.org.br/web/publicacoes/discussao/textos/texto_03_2007.pdf.

11 See, e.g., John Marshall, 2009, 'One size fits all? IMF tax policy in sub-Saharan Africa', Christian Aid Occasional Paper 2; and Matti Ylönen, 2017, 'Policy diffusion within international organizations: A bottom-up analysis of International Monetary Fund tax work in Panama, Seychelles, and the Netherlands', *UNU-WIDER Working Paper* 2017/157.

12 The International Centre for Tax and Development (ICTD) was established in 2010 with funding from the UK and Norwegian governments. Led by Mick Moore at the Institute of Development Studies, the consortium also included Christian Aid where I was then working, and an early agreed priority was the creation of a new tax dataset. Wilson Prichard of the University of Toronto headed up the project and ensured its successful delivery despite many

painful discoveries about the degree of neglect of the data, while Andrew Goodall of Charles University, Prague also made a major contribution.

13 Alex Cobham, 2014, 'Bad tax data, bad tax research? Introducing the new Government Revenue Dataset', *Center for Global Development* blog: https://www.cgdev.org/blog/bad-tax-data-bad-tax-research-introducing-new-government-revenue-dataset.

14 Kyle McNabb and Wilson Prichard, 2016, 'The ICTD government revenue dataset: Still the best option for researchers', International Centre for Tax and Development blog: https://www.ictd.ac/blog/the-ictd-government-revenue-dataset-still-the-best-option-for-researchers/.

15 The roots of the Tax Justice Network lie further back. A pivotal year was that of the MDGs, 2000. Oxfam published a seminal paper on the threat posed by tax havens to development (Ruth Mayne and Jenny Kimmis, 2000, 'Tax havens: Releasing the hidden billions for poverty eradication', *Oxfam Briefing Paper*: https://oxfamilibrary.openrepository.com/bitstream/10546/114611/1/bp-tax-havens-010600-en.pdf), estimating a revenue cost of around $50 billion a year; and the UK government published a white paper, which noted international tax avoidance and evasion as threats to revenues, and hence to development (HM Government, 2000, 'Eliminating world poverty: Making globalisation work for the poor', White Paper on International Development, London: HM Stationery Office: https://webarchive.national archives.gov.uk/+/http:/www.dfid.gov.uk/Documents/publications/whitepaper2000.pdf). As luck would have it, my then boss at Oxford, Valpy FitzGerald (now a commissioner of the Independent Commission for the Reform of International Corporate Taxation), had some hand in both, and so, by extension, I did too. The Oxfam paper in particular sparked civil society engagement with the issues, including vibrant discussions at the European Social Forum. A key trigger, however, was an approach by three Jersey residents – Jean Andersson, Pat Lucas and Frank Norman – to the island's former economic adviser, John Christensen. Christensen had written his resignation by attacking the island's tolerance of corrupt money in an interview with the *Wall Street Journal* and moved to the UK not long after. From their

conversations, there emerged a commitment to launch the Tax Justice Network – not to change Jersey, but to change the world. The important early steps have been documented and subject to academic study elsewhere (e.g., https://www.taxjustice.net/5828-2/ and https://www.taxjustice.net/2016/11/11/tax-justice-network-transition/, and various papers by Len Seabrooke and Duncan Wigan of Copenhagen Business School cited there), but it is worth highlighting two key priorities that Christensen pursued alongside building the expert and activist network: media coverage, and the engagement of international development NGOs. On the media side, it was late 2007 before a major outlet splashed on tax justice: the *Guardian* ran a front-page story, resulting from a six-month investigation of the international banana trade supported by the Tax Justice Network, under the headline: 'Revealed: How multinational companies avoid the taxman' (Felicity Lawrence and Ian Griffiths, *he Guardian*, 6 November 2007: https://www.theguardian.com/business/2007/nov/06/19). The 'dog bites man' feel of the headline reflects just how little prior coverage of this issue there had then been. Over the following years, successive rounds of journalists passed through the Tax Justice Network's training scheme, many of them going on to work on important international stories such as the Panama Papers in collaborations such as the International Consortium of Investigative Journalists. The training scheme has been spun off into the independent Finance Uncovered, which continues to provide courses as well as delivering cross-border investigative journalism through its international network, uncovering abuses of financial secrecy around the world. Finance Uncovered is currently leading work on the data from asset declarations and tax returns of politicians and officials worldwide. On the NGO side, early adopters included War on Want, before Christian Aid and then ActionAid launched the first major campaigns on tax justice in 2008. The global financial crisis shifted the terms of public debate around the responsibilities of the financial sector, and austerity politics quickly drew attention to questions of tax compliance by major players. With Oxfam coming back to the issue soon after, and others increasingly supportive, the development INGO sector was able to lead the way in demanding political progress in a range of forums including UN bodies as well as the G20 and G8 groups of countries, the Bretton Woods institutions and the OECD.

16 'A tax target for post-2015', *Uncounted*, 27 February 2015: http://uncounted.org/2015/02/27/tax-target-post-2015/. See also 'Should tax targets for post-2015 be rejected?', *Uncounted*, 18 May 2015: http://uncounted.org/2015/05/1 8/should-tax-targets-for-post-2015-be-rejected/.

17 Nick Shaxson, 2015, 'World Bank president: Corporate tax dodging "a form of corruption"', *Tax Justice Network*: https://www.taxjustice.net/2015/10/02/world-bank-presiden t-corporate-tax-dodging-a-form-of-corruption/.

18 http://tanaforum.org/tana-2014/#Tana2014DiscussionPape rs.

19 Alex Cobham and Luke Gibson, 2016, 'Ending the era of tax havens: Why the UK government must lead the way', *Oxfam Briefing Paper*: https://policy-practice.oxfam.org.uk/ publications/ending-the-era-of-tax-havens-why-the-uk-gove rnment-must-lead-the-way-601121.

20 Paddy Carter and Alex Cobham, 2016, 'Are taxes good for your health?', *UNU-WIDER Working Paper* 171: https:// www.wider.unu.edu/publication/are-taxes-good-your-heal th.

21 ICRICT, 21 June 2017, 'The definition of illicit financial flows as part of Sustainable Development Goal 16', *Letter to UN Secretary-General António Guterres*, Bogotá: Independent Commission for the Reform of International Corporate Taxation: https://www.taxjustice.net/wp-content/ uploads/2013/04/ICRICT-21-June-2017.pdf. In the same month, I used the opportunity of addressing the ECOSOC Financing for Development Forum to raise the issue there, setting it in the context of the changing corruption narrative: TJN, 1 June 2017, 'Tax Justice Network warns at the UN against subversion of Sustainable Development Goals', *Tax Justice Network*: https://www.taxjustice.net/2017/06/01/sub version-sdg-16-4/; see also George Turner, 23 June 2017, 'UN must defend target to curtail multinational companies' tax abuse', *Tax Justice Network*: https://www.taxjustice.net/ 2017/06/23/un-must-defend-target-curtail-multinational-co mvpanies-tax-abuse/.

22 Maya Forstater, 2018, 'Illicit financial flows, trade

misinvoicing, and multinational tax avoidance: The same or different?', *CGD Policy Paper* 123: https://www.cgdev.org/sites/default/files/illicit-financial-flows-trade-misinvoicing-and-multinational-tax-avoidance.pdf.

23 Raymond Baker, 2005, *Capitalism's Achilles Heel: Dirty Money and How to Renew the Free-Market System*, Hoboken: Wiley, p. 11.

24 'Illicit financial flows', 2015, *Report of the High Level Panel on Illicit Financial Flows from Africa*, p. 23: http://repository.uneca.org/handle/10855/22695.

25 'Illicit financial flows', p. 65.

26 UN, 2013, 'A new global partnership: Eradicate poverty and transform economies through sustainable development', *Report of the High-Level Panel of Eminent Persons on the Post-2015 Development Agenda*, New York: United Nations, p. 10: https://www.un.org/sg/sites/www.un.org.sg/files/files/HLP_P2015_Report.pdf.

27 UN, 'A new global partnership', p. 55.

28 See http://taxtobacco.org for full details of the campaign and its success.

29 Paul McClean, 2016, 'Groups demand tobacco lobbyist stops claiming links: Nestlé and World Bank demand to be removed from website', *Financial Times*, 7 November: https://www.ft.com/content/c9d6e11a-a1bb-11e6-82c3-4351ce86813f.

30 Paul McClean, 2017, 'Big tobacco lobby group quits smoking industry', *Financial Times*, 22 May: https://www.ft.com/content/6ca7f490-3c73-11e7-821a-6027b8a20f23.

31 Dave Hartnett and Hafiz Choudhury, 2014, 'Tax administration priorities in emerging and frontier markets', ITIC Issues Paper, p. 1: http://web.archive.org/web/20171215123526/http://www.iticnet.org/images/TaxAdministrationPrioritiesInEmergingAndFrontierMarkets.pdf.

32 Hartnett and Choudhury, 'Tax administration priorities in emerging and frontier markets', pp. 2, 4.

33 For a full survey of estimates of illicit financial flows, including a critical review of methodologies and data, and a range of proposals for indicators, see Alex Cobham and Petr Janský, 2020, *Estimating Illicit Financial Flows: A Critical Guide to the Data, Methodologies and Findings*, Oxford: Oxford University Press.

Chapter 6: Inequality, Understated

1 Anthony Atkinson, 1973, 'On the measurement of inequality', reprinted from *Journal of Economic Theory* (1970), with non-mathematical summary, pp. 46–68, in Atkinson (ed.), *Wealth, Income and Inequality*, Harmondsworth: Penguin Education, pp. 66–68.

2 Anthony Atkinson, Thomas Piketty and Emmanuel Saez, 2011, 'Top incomes in the long run of history', *Journal of Economic Literature* 49(1), pp. 3–71. These results are in keeping with the earlier study of Anton Korinek, Johan Mistiaen and Martin Ravallion, 'Survey nonresponse and the distribution of income', *World Bank Working Paper* 3543, who find upward corrections of the Gini for the United States during the sample years 1998–2004 ranging from 3.39 to 5.74 percentage points (raising the Gini from around 0.45 to 0.49–0.50).

3 Sudhir Anand and Paul Segal, 2015, 'The global distribution of income', in A. Atkinson and F. Bourguignon (eds), *Handbook of Income Distribution*, vol. 2A. Amsterdam: Elsevier, pp. 935–977.

4 Alex Cobham, William Davis, Gamal Ibrahim and Andy Sumner, 2016 'Hidden inequality: How much difference would adjustment for illicit financial flows make to national income distributions?', *Journal of Globalization and Development* 7(2).

5 Alex Cobham and Andy Sumner, 2013, 'Putting the Gini back in the bottle? "The Palma" as a policy-relevant measure of inequality', *mimeo*, King's College London, 15 March; Alex Cobham and Andy Sumner, 2013, 'Is it all about the tails? The Palma measure of income inequality', Center for Global Development Working Paper 343, September; Alex Cobham and Andy Sumner, 2014, 'Is inequality all about the tails?: The Palma measure of income inequality', *Significance* 11(1), pp. 10–13.

6 Alex Cobham, Lukas Schlögl and Andy Sumner, 2016, 'Inequality and the tails: The Palma Proposition and ratio', *Global Policy* 7(1), pp. 25–36.

7 Gabriel Palma, 2011, 'Homogeneous middles vs. heterogeneous tails, and the end of the "Inverted-U": The share of

the rich is what it's all about', Cambridge Working Papers in Economics 1111, p. 1; and Palma, 2006, 'Globalizing inequality: "Centrifugal" and "centripetal" forces at work', DESA Working Paper 35, New York: UN Department of Economic and Social Affairs.

8 See, e.g., Jonathan Ostry, Andrew Berg and Charalambos Tsangarides, 2014, 'Redistribution, inequality, and growth', IMF Staff Discussion Paper 14/02.

9 UN, 2013, 'A new global partnership: Eradicate poverty and transform economies through sustainable development', *Report of the High-Level Panel of Eminent Persons on the Post-2015 Development Agenda*, New York: United Nations, p. 16.

10 OWG, 2015, 'Open Working Group proposal for Sustainable Development Goals', New York: UN Open Working Group on Sustainable Development Goals: https://sustainabledevel opment.un.org/focussdgs.html.

11 Lars Engberg-Pedersen, 2013, 'Development goals post 2015: Reduce inequality', *DIIS Policy Brief*, Copenhagen: Denmark Institute for International Studies; Michael Doyle and Joseph Stiglitz, 2014, 'Eliminating extreme inequality: A Sustainable Development Goal, 2015–2030', *Ethics and International Affairs* 28(1); Alex Cobham, 2014, 'A solution for the inequality politics of post-2015?', *Center for Global Development*, 4 February; Post2015.org, 2013, 'Letter from leading academics addressed to High Level Panel says: Put inequality at the heart of post 2015!': https://web.archive. org/web/20150307111352/http://post2015.org/2013/03/21 /letter-from-leading-academics-addressed-to-high-level-pan el-says-put-inequality-at-the-heart-of-post-2015/.

12 World Bank, 2013, 'Shared prosperity: A new goal for a changing world', 8 May: http://www.worldbank.org/en/ news/feature/2013/05/08/shared-prosperity-goal-for-chan ging-world.

13 Sakiko Fukuda-Parr, 2019, 'Keeping out extreme inequality from the SDG agenda: The politics of indicators', *Global Policy* 10(S1), pp. 61–69.

Part III The Uncounted Manifesto

1 Nadia Saracini and Murali Shanmugavelan, on behalf of the BOND Caste and Development group, 2019, London: BOND; https://www.bond.org.uk/sites/default/files/resour ce-documents/bond_caste_reportscreen.pdf.

2 A heterosexual white man from an Anglophone, erstwhile imperial power, with parents who went to university, couldn't fit too many more intersecting inequalities on a Venn diagram. Globally speaking, I've been privileged to a quite unreasonable extent, but we all, including me, live worse lives because of all the inequalities in society. Feel your privilege, but don't beat yourself up about it – stand up and be counted, and help others to do the same.

3 The Poverty and Inequality Commission was formally set up from July 2019 as a new public body, as required by the Child Poverty (Scotland) Act 2017. The Act allows the Commission to set its own work programme in discussion with ministers, and to gather evidence, commission research and prepare reports. The Commission's specific roles include advising ministers on measures to reduce child poverty, scrutinising progress made towards the targets set out in the Act, monitoring progress in reducing poverty and inequality and promoting measures to ensure progress.

4 Open Data Watch, 2019, Open Data Inventory 2019: http:// odin.opendatawatch.com/.

5 Jonathan Gray, 2019, 'Data witnessing: Attending to injustice with data in Amnesty International's Decoders Project', *Information, Communication & Society* 22(7), pp. 971–991.

6 ICRICT, 2019, *A Roadmap for a Global Asset Registry: Measuring and Tackling Inequality: Curbing Tax Avoidance, Tax Evasion, Corruption and Illicit Financial Flows*, New York: Independent Commission for the Reform of International Corporate Taxation: https://www.icrict.com/ s/GAR.pdf.

Index

Note: Page numbers in *italic* refer to tables or figures in the text.